WHOSE STANDARDS?

WHOSE STANDARDS?

Consumer and Professional
Standards in Health Care

Charlotte Williamson

Open University Press
Buckingham · Philadelphia

Open University Press
Celtic Court
22 Ballmoor
Buckingham
MK18 1XW

and
1900 Frost Road, Suite 101
Bristol, PA 19007, USA

First Published 1992

A catalogue record of this book is
available from the British Library

Library of Congress Cataloging-in-Publication Data

Williamson, Charlotte
    Whose standards? Consumer and professional standards in health
care/Charlotte Williamson.
        p.   cm. – (State of health)
    Includes index.
    ISBN 0–335–09721–9 (hbk.)   ISBN 0–335–09720–0 (pbk.)
    1. Medical care – United States.   2. Consumer satisfaction.
I. Title.   II. Series: State of health series.
    [DNLM: 1. Consumer Advocacy.   2. Consumer Satisfaction.
3. Quality of Health Care.
W 84.1 W729w]
RA399.A3W55   1992
362.1′068′5 – dc20
DNLM/DLC
for Library of Congress   91–13012
                                                                 CIP

Typeset by Type Study, Scarborough
Printed in Great Britain by St Edmundsbury Press,
Bury St Edmunds, Suffolk

To Jack Hallas
and in memory of
Caireen Cruden

CONTENTS

SERIES EDITOR'S INTRODUCTION

Health services in many developed countries have come under critical scrutiny in recent years. In part this is because of increasing expenditure, much of it funded from public sources, and the pressure this has put on governments seeking to control public spending. Also important has been the perception that resources allocated to health services are not always deployed in an optimal fashion. Thus at a time when the scope for increasing expenditure is extremely limited, there is a need to search for ways of using existing budgets more efficiently. A further concern has been the desire to ensure access to health care of various groups on an equitable basis. In some countries this has been linked to a wish to enhance patient choice and to make service providers more responsive to patients as 'consumers'.

Underlying these specific concerns are a number of more fundamental developments which have a significant bearing on the performance of health services. Three are worth highlighting. First, there are demographic changes, including the ageing population and the decline in the proportion of the population of working age. These changes will both increase the demand for health care and at the same time limit the ability of health services to respond to this demand.

Second, advances in medical science will also give rise to new demands within the health services. These advances cover a range of possibilities, including innovations in surgery, drug therapy, screening and diagnosis. The pace of innovation is likely to quicken as the end of the century approaches, with significant implications for the funding and provision of services.

Third, public expectations of health services are rising as those

who use services demand higher standards of care. In part, this is
stimulated by developments within the health service, including the
availability of new technology. More fundamentally, it stems from
the emergence of a more educated and informed population, in
which people are accustomed to being treated as consumers rather
than patients.

Against this background, policymakers in a number of countries
are reviewing the future of health services. Those countries which
have traditionally relied on a market in health care are making
greater use of regulation and planning. Equally, those countries
which have traditionally relied on regulation and planning are
moving towards a more competitive approach. In no country is
there complete satisfaction with existing methods of financing and
delivery, and everywhere there is a search for new policy instruments.

The aim of this series is to contribute to debate about the future of
health services through an analysis of major issues in health policy.
These issues have been chosen because they are both of current
interest and of enduring importance. The series is intended to be
accessible to students and informed lay readers as well as to
specialists working in this field. The aim is to go beyond a textbook
approach to health policy analysis and to encourage authors to
move debate about their issue forward. In this sense, each book
presents a summary of current research and thinking, and an
exploration of future policy directions.

Professor Chris Ham
Director of the Health Services Management Centre,
University of Birmingham

PREFACE

There is confusion in the health service over a set of words in constant use – 'consumer', 'consumerism' and 'standards'. They, and related terms, like 'professional' and 'quality', are used with many meanings, some contradictory or trivial. There is also confusion, though it sometimes appears as discord rather than as muddle, over what are 'lower' and 'higher' standards for treatment and care, and about the criteria used to tell one from the other. These difficulties are partly due to different perspectives, themselves in part the result of differences in power, interest and position. But they are also due to lack of a theoretical framework for understanding consumerism and what standards consumers value.

This book puts forward a theoretical framework for understanding consumerism in health care and its relation to professionalism. From that follows a framework for understanding why many consumers and consumerists, and some professionals, intuitively perceive some standards as 'lower' or 'higher' than others. Elucidation of the principles underlying the standards that many consumers and consumerists think desirable helps us understand the depth and seriousness of their concerns. It also clears the way for a more fundamental and coherent approach throughout the service to standards and 'quality' than has so far been possible.

The discussion will be in this order. Chapter 1 provides a theoretical framework for understanding consumerism in terms of interests. Professionals' belief that they act in patients' best interests conflicts with consumerists' belief that patients can often act in their own best interests. But professional ideology can accommodate new definitions of best interests. Then professionals gradually come to accept some consumerist standards for treatment and care. The stages follow in that sequence partly because professionals have been established far longer than consumerists. But they follow in that sequence also because professionals have most of the power to define patients' interests. So consumerists, uncovering and redefining patients' interests, almost always have to act against the status quo. This chapter also defines the terms used in the discussion.

Chapter 2 is about consumerists and consumer groups and their ideologies and standards. Consumerists set a high value on consumers' autonomy, though that autonomy can include freely-chosen dependency. Chapter 3 discusses how far consumerist standards (those articulated by consumerist groups, and some self-help groups and avante guard professionals) match or represent those that 'ordinary' consumers hold. It separates consumerist general core standards from consumerist specialist standards in order to explore the question.

Chapter 4 defines the consumerist core standard of autonomy and names the six facets of that autonomy: respect, support, information, control, choice and decision-making. The argument that respecting and supporting patients' autonomy can be therapeutic is expanded from Chapter 2, in preparation for references to specific examples in the next six chapters.

Chapter 5, Respect, analyses the tasks practitioners and patients each have to do during episodes of treatment and care and suggests that respect lies at the heart of doing them well. Many low standards can be seen as related to lack of respect for patients, both as people and as objects of practitioners' work. Chapter 6, Support, describes some of the professional and institutional standards that consumerists have been least satisfied with and have worked hardest to change. Chapter 7, Information, discusses the apparently intractable conflict between professional and consumerist standards for offering information to patients. But it gives examples of professional good practice. Chapter 8, Control, also looks at some struggles but again notes examples of professional good practice. Chapter 9, Choice, shows how some consumerist groups and some professionals have tried to increase consumers' choices. Chapter 10 is about the controversial issue of clinical decision-making.

Chapter 11 recapitulates trends in standards. The opportunities offered by the government's introduction of specifications for service agreements are evident. But these opportunities will make exacting demands on everyone concerned with standards and with the specifications.

Chapter 12 brings the book to an optimistic conclusion. Conflicts between professionals' and consumers' interests will never disappear. But compatibilities or synergies of interest increase between professionals and consumers, as standards of treatment and care move from lower to higher levels, even though ultimate synergy can never quite be reached.

ACKNOWLEDGEMENTS

It is with great pleasure that I thank those who have spent time discussing the difficulties of raising standards of treatment and care with me. Some of these conversations took place just once, others over many years; each has given me insights and strengthened my purposes in writing this book. I am especially grateful to Mrs Peg Belson, Mrs Elizabeth Fradd, Mrs Elisabeth Hartley, Mrs Nancy Hill, Dr Peter Kennedy, Dr Tim Moss, Miss Maureen Oswin, and Dr David Wilkinson.

I am also most grateful to those who answered my questions by post or telephone or gave me references. They are many, but I want particularly to thank Ms Ingrid Baker, Ms Lynn Batehup, Ms Beverley Lawrence Beech, Mr David Chadwick, Ms Maggie Clifton, Mr J. Michael Dixon, Dr Lesley Fallowfield, Dr Pamela Fox-Russell, Mrs Sheila Gatiss, Mr John Henderson, Mrs Helen Hodgson, Ms Elizabeth Key, Dr Alison Kitson, Dr Shirley McIver, Mrs Nancy Mrozinski, Mr Peter Nicklin, Mr Malcolm Palmer, Mr John Porter, Dr D. L. Scott, Mr Martyn Smith, Dr Sue Sullivan, Ms Susan Waterworth, Dr Robert Wheatley, Mrs Joan Woodward and Dr T. Van Zwanenberg. I also thank Dr C. K. Drinkwater for permission to reproduce part of the Adelaide Medical Centre's primary health care team manifesto; Age Concern for permission to draw on their leaflet *Basic Principles for Working with Older People who Need Care*; and the editor of the *Health Education Journal* for permission to reproduce part of the table on literature on breast disorders that forms Table 9.3.

My husband, Professor Mark Williamson, read the complete draft. All the chapters in the book have also been read by a consumerist, Dr Priscilla Alderson, and a professional, Dr Gerry

Jackson. They gave time and thought generously and made many valuable comments and suggestions. To them I am deeply and gladly indebted.

INTERESTS AND IDEOLOGIES

Medicine is fundamentally a craft in which scientific knowledge is applied to particular patients for the purpose of right and good healing actions.

Doctor (1987)[1]

If these services are for our own good, why do we feel so bad about them?

Patient (1990)[2]

INTRODUCTION

One day the sacred snake of medicine unwound himself from Aesculapius' staff and bit a daughter of Eve. Her anger was stronger than her fear of sickness or her dependence upon the snake's master to cure her of it. Filling her basket with unripe apples from the tree of knowledge of concordant and discordant interests, she walked away from the magical security of believing that the snake's master would always do what was best for her. Then she sought a new order between herself and him.

Sickness saps energy and replaces peace of mind with anxiety. But it is only recently that health care itself has come to be widely seen as in some ways detrimental to some patients' interests. In the past there were harsh and harmful treatments and extreme inequities in sick people's access to health care. But the interests of health care professionals in treating illness, injury or disability and of patients in receiving treatment were seen as in accord with each other. Doctors and nurses did their best for each patient; the definition of what that best was, was left to them. Patients took that for granted. Sophisticated patients held that they freely handed over their authority and responsibility for themselves to their doctors and nurses during episodes of illness.[3] Naive ones simply accepted the way things were. There were disagreements and dissatisfactions in individual relationships, as well as confidence and good feeling. There were occasional accounts of poor care or dismal institutions. A few innovative and controversial individuals stood out against current professional practices. Novelists and playwrites from time to time wrote about nurses or doctors scornfully. But there was no social movement that sought to separate patients' interests from professionals' along lines of conflict or to challenge professionals to change their practice to accord with patients' views of their own interests.

The social movement that is changing this is the consumer movement or consumerism in health care. It began 40 to 50 years ago when a shift in widely accepted sets of values seems to have taken place across Europe and North America, weakening people's faith in authority in general.[4] Its origins are difficult to trace. But it showed itself in at least two ways in attitudes towards health care. Especially in the USA, sociologists increased the sharpness (both the clarity and the acerbity) of their analyses of health-care professions and institutions. They showed that professionals lost some of the ordinary 'lay' values during their training and early practice and were motivated, like everyone else, by self-interest at least as much as by altruism.[5] Large hospitals seemed to have some malign effects on patients, and to be run for staff's benefit more than patients'.[6] These perceptions offered the reading public amazing and unpleasing insights into familiar and unfamiliar places and happenings. At about the same time, in this country as well as America, patients or patients' relatives began to get together in groups to press for changes in the professional and institutional practices that angered them. Such pressure groups gave patients a voice. They were successful in changing some policies and practices, and grew in numbers and confidence.

These three elements – the creation of a climate of scepticism, the popularization of disturbing insights about professionals and institutions and the intense concern of small groups of patients or relatives – together contributed to the change in social consciousness we call consumerism in health care.

INTERESTS, KNOWLEDGE AND POWER

Consumerism in health care is often discussed in terms of knowledge or power, as if it were consumerism in commerce. I think that looking at consumerism in health care in terms of interests offers a more liberating analysis. It allows the dynamics of the convergences, conflicts and interchanges between consumerism and professionalism to be understood with sympathy towards both sides. It recognizes that though people sometimes lack power or knowledge, they always have interests; and that, when their interests are met, they do not need to secure them through knowledge or power. It takes account of the existential and not merely the political weakness of patients. And it makes prominent the idea that sometimes interests are suppressed, so that they are not known to the people who hold them.

Interests are to do with advantage and detriment, to individuals and to groups. Interests are difficult to define but are something in which a stake is held; a personal or group resource or means to protect or enhance a resource. Everyone has interests in resources like influence, power, time, money, knowledge, the way situations involving themselves are defined, how words are used about them and in a host of other material and immaterial things and in the relationships between them. Everyone has interests in health care, in its accessibility, its quality in general, and its standards of treatment and care.

Although interests are difficult to define, how they relate to each other and to the people who hold them can be described. I shall start from three points, put forward by Robert R. Alford in his structural theory of interests in health care, and will develop a new analysis of those interests and of the links between them. His points are that interests can be compatible or incompatible, synergistic or non-synergistic, with or between each other. Some interest-holders' interests can prevail over others' so regularly that they can be called dominant, those prevailed over being called repressed. And interests, though usually tied to interest-holders, are not always so tied.[7]

Synergistic and non-synergistic interests

All individuals and all groups of people have some interests that are the same as other people's in the sense of being entirely compatible with them, concordant with them, or working together with them, synergistic. They also have interests that conflict or are non-synergistic. (And they have some interests that are independent of each other.) This is as much so between distant nations as between close partners. Whose and which interests are synergistic or non-synergistic depends both on the nature of the issue and on the exact way it is defined, for definitions partly determine what is perceived and what is believed. The higher and more abstract the level at which an issue is defined, the more likely people's interests in it will be synergistic. So people express more satisfaction with the health service in general than with the details of the care they have received in it. The greater the collective belief that everyone's interests are synergistic, the greater the social harmony.

At lower levels of analysis, and particularly the one that concerns us, that of treatment and care, conflicts of interest or lack of synergy become more conspicuous. Different interests can be seen to be more closely tied to different interest-holders. That is because individuals' own experiences lead them to see that their interests are different from other people's, particularly if they have some means of comparison or analysis to hand. Even such a simple thing as happening to know that there is more than one way of doing things can provide that means.

■ 'Why is it that in other towns, visiting is open from lunch time until evening?' was the comment of a patient answering a questionnaire about short visiting times in a hospital in 1987.[8]

At the level of treatment and care, conflicts of interest are usually between individual patients or categories of patients and individual practitioners or categories of practitioners – professionals in direct relationships with patients. But the personal still reflects the social: the more strongly practitioner and patient believe that each's interests are synergistic with the other's, the greater the trust between them. Synergistic interests bind people and society together. They are like ripe and rosy apples for everyone to pick.

Dominant and repressed interests

The medical profession and the professions related to it (nursing as a profession in its own right and the paramedical professions like physiotherapy and radiography) are said to have dominant interests because their interests, collective and individual, tend to prevail over those of patients and other lay people in the health service. The health-care professions are long-established, strong and cohesive. In each profession there is a basis of common knowledge and perception and an understanding of the interests that all members share. Though the other health professions often resent doctors' power *vis-à-vis* themselves, they are inclined to exercise similar power over the recipients of their care. In their relationships with those recipients and in their practice, professionals are largely self-regulating. All have exceptional power to define their patients' situation and their interests:

> To be a professional simply is, in large part, to have been granted the authority to create by one's own pronouncements what counts as true and what counts as false about a certain subject.[9]

This dominance in the creation and use of concepts and percepts is supported by the health professions', especially the medical profession's, broader power in society. Power can be defined as the means to secure one's own interests in desired stakes or resources. There is a circularity of argument about professionals' power, because securing their interests in any one resource enhances their resources to obtain others. So it is difficult to decide whether it is professionals' power that leads society to believe that professionals, especially doctors, are valuable and that their definitions and interests should prevail; or whether it is society's belief in professionals' value that leads it to grant them their powers.[10] Probably both beliefs interact and reinforce each other. But whatever the origins of professional dominance, it is well established.

Once professionals' dominant interests are established, recipients' interests can be said to be repressed. Repressed interests can be synergistic with dominant interests. That is implicit in the paragraph on synergistic and non-synergistic interests, and is an important point. Every group of dominant interest-holders tries to persuade other people that their interests are synergistic with its own; that is a crucial way it seeks to sustain its power. Nevertheless, there are many synergisms between dominant and repressed interests, those of professionals and those of recipients in health care, whatever the level of analysis.

■ When someone with a cut hand goes to the doctor for treatment, and the doctor treats it effectively (so that the wound heals without distortion of the tissues and the patient suffers no short- or long-term hazards like infection), both patient's and doctor's interests are synergistic. The patient's interests are in his or her use of the hand and immediate and

future health. The doctor's interests are in being a competent practitioner, able to affect the patient's welfare for the better, and justly
earning the emotional, social and financial rewards of his or her
knowledge and skill.

This is the ideal type of clinical encounter or episode of care. It is
satisfactory to both parties and fosters good feeling between them.
Any differences of power between them are immaterial. The
doctor's professional and legal powers, to assess and define the
severity of the wound, to stitch it, and to prescribe an antibiotic or
tetanus injection if necessary, are put to positive use for the
patient's benefit. The patient's part in deciding that the cut was
serious enough to go to the doctor but not serious enough to go to an
Accident and Emergency Department, and in having a reasonably
accurate idea of what the treatment ought to be, is powerful though
inconspicuous. Neither goes beyond his or her competence nor fails
within it through carelessness, arrogance or ignorance.[11] Histori-
cally, most episodes of care or encounters between patients and
practitioners have been seen as like this. Many are like this
(however rigorously and thoroughly the episodes or encounters are
analysed) every day and all over the western world.

When, however, repressed interests are not synergistic with
dominant interests, they can be non-synergistic in either of two
ways. They can be oppressed or suppressed. Interests are oppressed
when the (repressed) interest-holders (as individuals or groups)
perfectly recognize and can define clearly their own interests in an
issue, but dominant interest-holders prevent them from meeting
those interests or having them met. Often the struggle is plain to
see: the oppressed interest-holders feel frustration and anger, the
dominant-interest holders defiance and doubt. Then inequalities of
power (power in the sense of being able to secure something one
wants) between oppressed and dominant interest-holders matter
greatly. Consumer pressure groups, working for changes in standards of treatment and care, are usually started by oppressed
interest-holders.

■ In the 1960s and 1970s many mothers intended to feed their babies 'on
demand' (the babies' demand) in maternity units. They felt that prompt
and loving responsiveness was right, both for the babies' comfort and for
their development into loving adults. For mothers who wanted to
breast-feed, there was the additional reason that breast-feeding (with
its nutritional and immunological benefits to babies) is most easily

established when suckling stimulates the production of milk in accordance with the babies' appetites. But many midwives believed that babies should be fed at regular intervals by the clock. They had concerns about babies getting enough milk and about protecting mothers' nipples from too frequent or too long suckling. Some also believed that babies should be disciplined from birth and not 'spoilt'.

So mothers' interests in their babies' health and welfare conflicted with midwives' interests in maintaining order and control in the wards (knowing that all the babies had been fed the right number of feeds per day and controlling the periods of suckling) and in their view of themselves as the trained experts in baby care who knew best. Midwives generally won the struggle, from their position of institutionally-supported control, though some midwives turned a blind eye to babies being fed at the wrong time or smuggled babies from the nursery to their mothers.

In 1976 a new standard for maternity care, recommending 'flexibility' in feeding, was promoted by the Department of Health in response to leading professional opinion and pressure from consumer groups.[12] At first this official guidance was widely disregarded.[13] In 1985 the standard was strengthened to 'Demand feeding should be encouraged whether the baby is breast or bottle fed.'[14] By the 1980s the new standard was accepted by most midwives and maternity units and incorporated into routine practice. The long and painful conflicts over the issue, however, left bitter feelings in some maternity pressure groups and some mothers.

Interests are suppressed when dominant interest-holders manage issues in such a way that the groups or individuals whose interests are at risk of harm are not even aware that there is an issue at stake.[15] Then they cannot speak up or make demands on their own account. Very often other people who might feel concern about the issue are also precluded from knowledge of it. Secrecy is an obvious means by which individuals' and groups' interests are suppressed in all sorts of human activity. To do something in secret is to suppress knowledge of it, and therefore to suppress the interests of people who might be affected by it. But recipients' interests can also be suppressed when medicine's and nursing's own scientific approaches and changing knowledge are brought to bear slowly (or not at all) on certain issues. Inequalities of power (in the sense above) between suppressed and dominant interest-holders are not immediately relevant in direct relationships between individual suppressed interest-holders and individual dominant interest-holders. By definition, suppressed interest-holders do not know there is something they should be asking for or expecting. Individual dominant interest-holders may feel unease or guilt. But guilt can be diminished or disowned by blaming other people or by giving greater priority to considerations other than the particular patient's welfare.

■ Some consultants have put age limits on patients' eligibility for life saving but expensive treatments like thrombolytic treatment for myocardial infarction.[16] This rationing has not been made widely known. Neither people living in the hospitals' catchment areas, who might become patients, nor patients themselves as they come into hospital expecting treatment after a heart attack, have usually been aware of it. So they have been unable to ask to be sent to a hospital without such a policy. Their interests in living or dying, and in knowing about the situation in which they have, or might, find themselves, have been suppressed.

Doctor's interests here have lain in upholding collegiate solidarity by cooperating with each other in sharing resources between different specialties.[17] The policy was justified by the belief that older patients were too decrepit to undergo the treatment's risks. But research has shown that some elderly patients benefit as much or more than younger ones from treatment.[18] Even before that research, the different ages used as the cut-off point for treatment cast doubt upon the reasons for it. The form rationing took was unquestionably supported by widespread ageism inside and outside the health service. Moreover, there was the comforting thought that elderly patients would prefer to die of a heart attack than to live longer and risk suffering from degenerative or malignant diseases. But whatever the merits of these ideas, elderly patients' interests were repressed by the secrecy of the policies that acted against them; by the application of a policy to them all instead of the individual assessment of their clinical condition that is supposed to guide clinical decisions; and by the lack of an opportunity for them to express their own values and wishes, that followed from the secrecy.

Consumer pressure groups cannot be started by suppressed interest-holders. But established consumer groups can uncover suppressed interests and so convert their status to that of oppressed interests. Of course health professionals themselves are in a better position to do that than consumer groups. Sometimes they do, either by acting directly or by alerting a consumer pressure group.

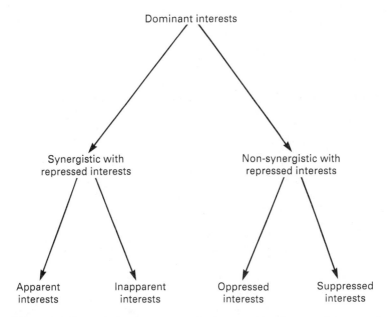

Figure 1.1 Synergies and non-synergies between dominant and repressed interests.

Figure 1.1 is a diagram of interests and their synergies and non-synergies. I have explained my use of the terms oppressed and suppressed interests. Synergistic interests that repressed interest-holders can see for themselves (or know) are met, I shall call apparent.

■ When a dentist puts on sterile gloves in front of a patient, the patient can see that the dentist is protecting both parties' interests in being safeguarded against infection.

Inapparent synergistic interests are interests met, though the repressed interest-holder cannot see or may not know about them.

■ A nurse who pulls a sheet over a naked unconscious patient, as protection from the embarrassment that he or she would feel, if conscious, meets the patient's interest in retaining dignity.

Many professional standards articulate and promote apparent or inapparent synergistic interests. Breaches of these standards are errors, or they are bad practice due to poor training, excessive stress or shortcomings in systems or their organization.[19] But there is no disagreement between professionals and anyone else about what is 'good' and 'bad'.

Even these few examples illustrate the complexity that surrounds issues to do with standards of care and treatment. Most standards are synergistic between dominant interest-holders and repressed interest-holders. That is so whether the interests are apparent or inapparent. Non-synergistic interests, oppressed or suppressed, are controversial. Strong feelings, multiple motivations and eclectic explanations and rationalizations are the ground upon which the conflicts are fought. But deep feelings direct the hope in us all that synergistic interests will be common and non-synergistic rare.

Interest-holders and interests

Interests are not strictly tied to groups or categories of interest-holders. They cannot be, because although some interests are material, others are ideas, beliefs or perceptions, and they are by their nature unbound. But training, experience and situation guide people towards particular ideas and particular perceptions of their own and other people's interests. So all groups hold some ideas rather than others. Nevertheless, individual interest-holders or groups may change their perceptions of what their interests are. Some doctors, midwives and nurses can remember exactly when they were suddenly converted to an oppressed interest-holder's view on a specific issue. At that moment, they changed their mind. That everyday metaphor captures such a change's import. Professionals who change their minds have to reconstruct their ideas of what being a good professional means. Conversely, some lay people who work in the consumer movement feel more aligned with professionals than with consumers.[20] They support the formers' interests when they are in conflict with the latters'. Or they fail to distinguish interests from each other accurately. Dominant interests are just that – dominant – because most lay as well as professional people support them, or at least do not actively oppose them.

That interests are not permanently attached to interest-holders is important because it means that interests can shift and change. Suppressed interests become oppressed interests, if the suppression is disclosed but the interests remain unmet. Oppressed interests become synergistic interests when professionals alter their standards to meet consumers' interests. Quite small alterations in meanings – a hint from a nurse to relative, a note in an obscure journal – can make major differences to how interests are perceived. Those perceptions can lead to major changes in standards.

Both oppressed and suppressed interests are a moral and political challenge to consumerism and to professionalism. They sometimes fail that challenge's test. Yet they cannot live up to their purposes and their ideals until they pass it.

THE CONSUMER MOVEMENT

The consumer movement is concerned with the four kinds of repressed interests: apparent and inapparent, oppressed and suppressed. The variety and diffuseness of the movement's efforts can obscure what it does. Those who oppose dominant interests often adopt protective camouflage or hide the green and yellow apples in their baskets under the red ones, to disarm dominant interest-holders' suspicion. So people in the consumer movement talk about 'improving the health service', just as professionals do. Both suit their definitions of improvements to themselves. Nevertheless, all the kinds of endeavour can be seen in the consumer movement:

- Almost every individual or group at some time works to promote recipients' interests that are synergistic with providers': asking the government for more resources; raising money from the public; talking about better training for paramedical professionals or shorter hours for junior doctors.
- Many individuals and groups also work to promote oppressed interests: to secure acceptance of new standards of care; to 'empower' patients to make choices; to support oppressed interest-holders in their complaints or battles.
- Some individuals and groups, a minority, work for recipients' suppressed interests. They try to make what was seen as 'natural' and taken for granted come to be seen as strange and unacceptable. They try to alter our sensibilities and values. They try to uproot our assumptions and beliefs. They remind us that dominant interests, and the social structures that support them, can prevent people from knowing what their own interests are in certain situations.[21] In this they are radical; and because of their work, the consumer movement is partly a radical movement.

Radical and partly radical movements, dealing with ideas like interests, are liable to run into confusion, their own and other people's, when it comes to transferring abstractions to categories of people. Who are the consumers of health care? Can they be identified by some personal or social attribute they all have, or do they have to hold particular beliefs? Whose are the standards that can be compared and contrasted with those that professionals hold?

Comparing consumerism with another radical movement, feminism, helps us answer these questions. Feminists are women and men who hold particular ideas about the disadvantage of women *vis-à-vis* men in our society. They deal in non-synergistic interests, oppressed and suppressed. They hold various shades of opinion, but in the main their object is to identify and promote women's interests until they are met as unquestioningly and regularly as men's. So feminists' constituents are women, both a biological category, and a social one in their institutionalized relation to men. The category 'woman' is a life-long one. It can be reasonably extended to baby girls as yet unborn and to women who were once alive. But men cannot be included in the category, woman; and is not to women's advantage when men pretend that all men's and women's interests are 'really' the same.

Feminists' equivalents in consumerism are sometimes called 'consumer advocates'. 'Consumerists' is a better term because advocate has various meanings in health care. Health professionals who support some oppressed or suppressed interests are the equivalent of male feminists. Like them, they understand and even give a lead on some issues, but seldom entirely change over to become a sort of woman or sort of deprofessional. Consumerists' constituents, consumers, are the recipients of health care.

Consumers – the recipients of health care – are patients or users of the service. Patienthood, unlike womanhood, is usually a temporary condition. And unlike womanhood, everyone has a passport to the kingdom of the sick.

■ Illness is the night-side of life, a more onerous citizenship. Everyone who is born holds dual citizenship, in the kingdom of the well and the kingdom of the sick. Although we all prefer to use only the good passport, sooner or later each of us is obliged, at least for a spell, to identify ourselves as citizens of that other place.[22]

Thus health professionals are consumers of health care for the duration of their sickness or their use of the service, just as lay

Table 1.1   Pairs of terms

dominant interest-holder	repressed interest-holder
professional	consumer
practitioner	patient
proto-professional	consumerist

people are. Patients' and users' close relatives or carers are included in the category provided that they have authority to act on behalf of the patient or user. The category 'consumer' can also reasonably be extended to former and future recipients of health care. But when it is, it must be in reference to the recipient–provider relationship or situation.

The word 'patient' is so rich in history and meaning that it deserves to be kept. In this book I shall use the words 'professional' and 'consumer' in a general sense and 'practitioner' and 'patient' when I am thinking of the direct or clinical relationship between individual professionals and individual consumers. Consumerists' equivalents amongst professionals I shall call 'proto-professionals'; the reasons are given in the next section. Table 1.1 summarizes these usages.

Neither all women nor all consumers believe they are disadvantaged *vis-à-vis* men or *vis-à-vis* professionals. But to others the very word 'woman' or 'patient' conveys a sense of the inauspicious. What individuals believe depends upon their knowledge, their experience, their temperament, their styles of coping with adversity and the extent to which they find confirmation or denial of their perceptions amongst their peers. Often it is only personal experience that convinces a woman that women are disadvantaged *vis-à-vis* men or a patient that patients' interests are second to practitioners'. And even bad experiences may be interpreted (wrongly or rightly) as accidental or exceptional, unconnected to the general pattern of events. This variability in perception and belief does not invalidate the categories as defined. To be a woman or a patient is not to make a free doctrinal choice. Naturally feminists and consumerists would like all their constituents to be more aware of their potential disadvantages than many are. Equally naturally, dominant interest-holders are always hoping to come across large random samples of perfectly contented women or consumers.

Again, just as there are things about women and men that cannot be changed, so there are about patients and practitioners. Patients need help that they cannot give themselves and practitioners do not need that help. Avoiding becoming a patient in the first place (through preventive or prophylactic care), or through self care, or through seeking help from non-professionals, are common strategies for escaping from this unfortunate circumstance. But they do not always suffice. Some people, as well as looking out their passport to the kingdom of the sick, read up about their diagnosed or probable condition and its treatments, discover what they can about local doctors' reputations, and try to find or negotiate what they consider the best treatment and care for themselves. They can be called 'active patients'. They are seen as the ideal type of consumer by some consumerists. (Practitioners, conversely, can see them as the dread type – the demanding patient.) But the biological imperatives of illness, injury and the onset of disability cannot be done away with. Disease, the cause of illness, and illness, the psycho-physiological manifestation of disease, can only be re-defined socially up to a point. We can understand them in ways that change with our changing knowledge. We can place different social values and meanings on them – stigma or romance, odium or indifference.[23] But we cannot deny that disease exists. Moreover, even an active patient cannot discuss loss of blood or prophylaxis against clotting whilst under a general anaesthetic, or debate treatment in a sudden emergency. And many patients are never able even to begin to protect their own interests in treatment and care: the very young, the very frail old, the severely demented. Then too, certain sorts of knowledge, essential to the role of active patient or ideal consumer, may be unwelcome to some patients, unhelpful to their coping strategies. Lowered energy and lack of physical technical ability to treat or care for themselves (though not necessarily lack of knowledge) characterize patients. That is the way things are; and there are therefore limits to the extent to which patients can be energized or directly and individually 'empowered'.

The limitations to 'empowering' patients that the biological exigencies of illness and injury impose mean that some repressed interests need special protection. This is recognized through statutory regulations to protect consumers' interests. Some consumerists try to get those interests embodied as rights. But rights can never apply to more than a minority of issues and situations. So consumerists have to work most of the time by articulating and promoting standards that would benefit categories of consumers and individual consumers, whatever the state of their health and the legal status of their interests.

Standards are sometimes made compulsory by law; but much more often they are gradually incorporated into policies and practices that professionals come to accept as their own, compatible with their own interests. In that sense, the work of consumerists can be said to consist of identifying oppressed and suppressed interests and trying to turn them into synergistic ones.

STANDARDS

In themselves, standards are merely qualitative or quantitative measures to which values can be assigned. Care and treatment in the health service in all its aspects – diagnosis, treatment, preventive, recuperative, rehabilitative and palliative care – can be thought of as given through a series or cluster of actions or practices. Almost all the environmental, interpersonal and technical aspects of practices can be made the subject of standards. Anything that can be put into words can be assigned a value. Some things cannot be put into words. They are too delicate or too complex or have no words yet to express them. But theoretically, virtually every aspect of care and treatment can be identified and measured and set quantitative or qualitative standards. In fact, relatively few aspects are identified. But the number of standards it is possible to set increases as our ability to define and measure aspects of treatment and care, especially process and outcome, improves.[24] What is considered as good or bad, acceptable or unacceptable, changes over time in the light of changing social, professional, and, within the last 40 years or so, consumerist values and interests.

Both professionals and consumerists work to see standards improved – improved according to their own values and their own criteria:

● A consumer standard of treatment or care is a standard that promotes the interests of consumers, as consumerists define those interests, in the practice or issue to which it applies.
● A professional standard for treatment or care is a standard that

promotes the interests of consumers, as most professionals define those interests, in the practice or issue to which it applies.

These definitions apply equally to synergistic and non-synergistic interests. The definitions, though parallel, are worded differently. There are four categories of people who are relevant here: consumerists and 'ordinary' consumers, professional opinion leaders and 'ordinary' professionals. Why are consumers not equivalent to professionals? The asymmetry follows from our discussion of non-synergistic interests.

The first reason is that work on standards that protect or promote consumers' interests has to be done by consumerists; it is they who are in a position to share knowledge and experience and to identify oppressed and suppressed interests. Individual consumers of course make judgments all the time – everyone does. But the next step, casting those judgements into standards and promoting them, generally requires support from other people. Individual consumers who seek that support, to define their own interests more clearly and to generalize and extend their own thoughts and feelings, become (by definition) consumerists. So consumer standards are consumerist standards, while consumers' standards are those individual consumers hold. Individual professionals, by contrast, are usually clear about their own interests. From their training and in their professional meetings and publications they identify and sustain a corporate or collegiate view of them. This can be seen whenever something new is proposed to professionals; there is an immediate mobilization of opinion and response. 'Ordinary' consumers usually lack the networks and the communality of knowledge that would equate them to 'ordinary' professionals.

The second reason is that when consumerists identify oppressed or suppressed interests, and promote standards that protect those interests, most consumers usually benefit, either immediately or in due course. (Dominant interest-holders like to believe that 'ordinary' or naive consumers judge treatment and care by criteria different from consumerists' criteria. They believe that consumerists are 'biased'. So they are; but so are the dominant interest-holders. Differences in judgement between consumerists and consumers, where they exist, are usually to do with degrees of familiarity with consumerists' concepts and percepts, not with fundamental divergencies of feeling or response. We shall look at this closely in Chapter 3. Oppressed interests to some extent (depending on how transparent the issue is to the individual interest-holder) and suppressed interests relate to what interest-holders would want to have, if they knew what the issues at stake were.) In contrast, when an innovative professional identifies an interest non-synergistic with dominant interests, and promotes a standard that protects or enhances that non-synergistic interest, he or she goes against dominant interests. So those new standards are resisted by most fellow professionals, just as they would be if they originated from consumerists.

These fellow professionals, as dominant interest-holders, have a lot at stake: familiar patterns of work; old skills; comfortable assumptions; institutionalized support or sanction; established relationships and patterns of communication with each other;[25] socio-psychological coping strategies and defence mechanisms;[26] convenience; status.[27] Resistance is so common that it seems normal; so common that change itself is often seen as creating resistance, in disregard of the speed with which professionals, like everybody else, accept change when it is to their advantage. So professional innovators' standards promoting interests non-synergistic with the majority of the profession are seldom accepted quickly. But a profession is its members; it can therefore be said that a professional standard is one accepted by most of the profession. Non-synergistic standards, formulated by innovative professionals, can be called proto-professional standards, until, when the majority accept them, they become professional standards. The innovative professionals can be called proto-professionals. The distinction may be difficult to draw pragmatically, because new standards are accepted erratically. Moreover, not every proto-professional takes a non-synergistic perspective on every issue, any more than every consumerist takes a radical view on every topic. But making the distinction is useful in understanding how new standards arise and diffuse. New non-synergistic standards come both from (proto) professionals and from consumerists.

When the majority of professionals have accepted a new standard into their practice, it becomes a professional standard whether it originated from consumerists or proto-professionals. That is the end for which consumerists work. Table 1.2 summarizes the main stages in the articulation of a non-synergistic standard and its acceptance as an agreed standard. When a non-synergistic standard becomes redefined and accepted by dominant interest-holders as a

Table 1.2   Stages in the articulation and acceptance of a new consumerist or proto-professional standard

Stage 1	Stage 2	Stage 3
consumers' repressed interests seen as synergistic by professionals and consumerists	consumers' interests identified as non-synergistic with professionals'	professionals accept consumers' interests as synergistic with theirs
no consumerist or proto-professional standard (sometimes no explicit professional standard)	professional standard threatened by proto-professional or consumerist standard	proto-professional or consumerist standard accepted as new professional or 'agreed' standard
harmony	conflict	harmony

synergistic one, harmony and good feeling replace anguish and suspicion.

Proto-professionals

The part professionals play in formulating standards that are non-synergistic with accepted professional interests is extremely important to consumerists and consumers. There seem to be two kinds of professionals who relinquish or redefine some aspect of the interests their peers uphold. The first kind includes opinion leaders in the medical and nursing professions. In their search for better treatments and patterns of care, they take up some consumerists ideas. Or they respond to consumers' requests or complaints, and incorporate that response into policy. Or they arrive at the same ideas in working on the scientific and craft bases of medicine and nursing. Every profession has innovators, part of whose skill is in picking up ideas and feelings from diverse sources. Though proto-professionals' and consumerists' starting points may be different, the conclusions they draw from them about standards of care and treatment are often the same.

These innovators' positions within their professions are apt to be unstable; they earn fame or ostracism. But in either case, they are important in starting debates and controversies from which new ideas, perceptions and standards come.

The second kind of health professional includes those who have had to use their passports to the kingdom of the sick. They have been patients. Or they have found themselves the relatives or close friends of patients. When they experience as consumers the detriments as well as the goods of health care, they can gain new perspectives. Their ability to assess standards of treatment and care by technical criteria, and by medicine's and nursing's own high ideals, adds special dimensions to their judgements. When they recover, they can take back new sympathies and insights to their practice. They may be able to influence colleagues; or work through their professional organizations to improve standards of treatment or care; or be a link between other professionals and consumerists. So their influence can be wide. But they, too, risk the stress that going against dominant interests entails.

Besides having allies in proto-professionals, consumerists have another, perhaps even more important, advantage in their work for non-synergistic interests. It is health professionals' own ideology of patient care. An ideology is a set of beliefs that serves both to express a group's aspirations and to justify its existence. Members of the medical profession, and of the professions that share its ethical basis, are committed to the ideal of doing their best for patients, to acting in those patients' best interests.[28] This commitment is partly self-serving, to do with maintaining a powerful place in society through its promise that its interests are synergistic with everyone else's. It is sometimes manifestly false, as when professionals keep quiet about colleagues' incompetent or dangerous practices.[29] Yet it is at the same time an exalted and humane hope. It is a promise that most of us think worth having. We rely on it for our security when we are well. We put trust in it when we are sick. It is also a remarkable commitment. (Men, to return to our comparison between women and consumers, do not commit themselves to act in the best interests of women, even as a touch of rhetoric or its cousin, cant.) And although medicine and the other health professions have accustomed themselves to defining what best is, they also have the power to change that definition.

It is a paradox that what gives the health professions their power to act against consumers' non-synergistic interests – their power to define what is best for consumers – also gives them the power to change to what consumerists and proto-professionals convince them is best.

Going against dominant interests is hard. Trying to persuade dominant interest-holders that their interests would be better served by standards of treatment and care that seem at first to go against their beliefs or accustomed ways of working is slow. The yellow and green apples of discord – oppressed and suppressed interests – are sharp to those who dare to pick them. They take a long time to ripen. But in the end they mostly do.

2

CONSUMERISTS

. . . everything begins in sentiment and assumption and finds its issue in political action and institutions. The converse is also true: just as sentiments become ideas, ideas eventually establish themselves as sentiments.

Lionel Trilling (1940)[1]

INTRODUCTION

There are many professional and consumer interest groups in this country. Professional groups range from the long-established and prestigious Royal Colleges of Medicine and Surgery to recent groups like the Primary Nursing Network (Oxford Region). They work to guide professional standards and practice, to facilitate mutual support and help among their members, and to advance their interests.

Consumer groups include national and local campaigning groups, primarily concerned with standards and the interests of specific care groups; self help groups; and 'mixed' groups, providing services, campaigning and facilitating mutual support among members.[2] So in some ways, professional and consumer groups are parallel. But professional groups are, on the whole, much more influential, as would be expected of dominant interest-holders. One difference between groups of dominant and of repressed interest-holders is important for the articulation and promotion of standards. Professional groups seldom have consumers or consumerists as members; but some consumer groups have professionals as members or advisers.

Added to groups on the consumer side, are Community Health Councils (CHCs). They are statutory bodies, set up in 1974, one in every health district. Their remit is to 'represent the community's interests in the NHS'.[3] So they cover consumers among the other citizens in their health districts.

Though their activities are diverse, all these groups are concerned, in some degree, with standards in health care. The Royal Colleges take a lead in articulating professional standards. Often, but not always, their standards are synergistic with consumers' interests. Amongst those that are synergistic, proto-professional standards can sometimes be found.

The variety of consumer groups also reflects their members' perception and espousal of interests. The consumer groups that work mainly or entirely for standards of treatment and care that are non-synergistic with professionals' interests, I shall call 'consumer pressure groups' or 'consumerist groups'. They include some groups with charitable status and some self help groups as well as some campaigning ones.

CONSUMER PRESSURE GROUPS

Consumer pressure groups seek to protect the interests of specific 'care groups', people who share a particular condition, disease, disability or predicament and who experience the professional or institutional care customary for it. They draw their members largely, but not exclusively, from their specific care group. The meanings they give to their personal experiences form part of the shared perceptions, ideas and sensibilities that each pressure group builds up as part of its specialized knowledge base.

The cardinal interest that consumer pressure groups work to protect is their constituents' freedom to act in their own best interests. Consumerists believe that people can act in their own best interests, or those of their dependents, from 'ordinary' intuitions, feelings and thought, in most situations. In special situations like sickness, people can still act in their own best interests if they have 'enough' information, preferably information from more than one source and from more than one perspective. (There are situations in which neither the consumer nor the professional know what the consumer's best interests are. Or the consumer's or the professional's view, or both, may be evidently wrong. These cases do not invalidate the consumerist argument. On the contrary, the uncertainty of medicine supports it.) So consumerists uphold consumers' self-determination or autonomy. That self-determination can include an autonomous choice of dependency, by those who wish to manage their sickness or predicament in that way. That is important. But to consumerists, imposed dependency is an evil. The distinction between freely-chosen dependency and imposed dependency is difficult to discern in practice – in a ward of apparently compliant and passive patients – for example. Just as professionals tend to see patients as more passive and ignorant than they are, so consumerists tend to see them as more active and knowledgable. 'Our imperfect capacity to comprehend reality,' to use a phrase of John Bowlby's,[4] unites consumerists and professionals. But autonomy or self-determination is none the less a fundamental value to consumerists.

CONSUMERISM AND PROFESSIONALISM

At first sight, the consumerist's position is not in conflict with many professionals' stated principles. Increasingly often, health-care professionals say they wish to respect patients' autonomy.[5] Professionals, however, are inclined to see autonomy as something bestowed or permitted by them. They do not see it, as consumerists do, as something that cannot be conferred by professionals, though it can be damaged by them. The difference is subtle. But it can be picked up by comparing how professionals and consumerists write. Professionals might refer to allowing patients in hospital to wear their own clothes. Consumerists would probably put the word 'allow' into sarcastic quotation marks.

More significantly, because deeper at the heart of professionalism, the consumerist position on autonomy is, in theory, not in conflict with professionals' idea of clinical autonomy or clinical freedom. Professionals are autonomous in matters of clinical care. Clinical care in a strict sense is the personal contract, usually implicit, between a patient and a practitioner, in which one asks for advice and the other gives it.[6] Clinical autonomy is the practitioner's freedom to offer such advice about diagnosis and treatment as his or her clinical judgement, based on knowledge and experience, suggests. Clinical autonomy or freedom to act in carrying out the advice derives from the patient's agreement, or informed consent, to it. So it rests on the patient's authority as much as on the practitioner's. When practitioner and patient reach a mutual agreement, there should be no intervention from outside the relationship. This right protects patients by enabling them and their practitioners to act together in the patient's best interests. Clinical freedom is never absolute.[7] Resources, past, present or future, may prevent practitioners from providing what would benefit some patients. Clinical guidelines and protocols (sets of standards for specific procedures) may exclude certain courses of clinical action that patients would prefer. Patients' complaints about treatment, if found justified by a third party, can bring censure on practitioners. Nevertheless, professional clinical autonomy derives from consumers' autonomy and authority, even when they choose to make an autonomous choice of dependency ('You do what you think is best, doctor.')

But in everyday health care, as distinct from ethical theory, things may be different. Consumers' autonomy is at risk in two ways. Within the individual clinical relationships between practitioners and patients, it is at risk from practitioners' genuine conviction that they know what patients' best interests are. This conviction is fed by complex sets of concepts and percepts that are not necessarily transparent to the practitioners themselves. Analysing patients' interests with them, even at a fairly superficial level, is time-consuming and often difficult. To do it thoroughly is extremely hard.

A patient's suppressed interests in a specific issue or practice (in what is done or not done) are, by definition, unknown to him or her. They may be unknown to the practitioner as well. (In any discussion of interests, there is a problem in distinguishing between what could not be known to someone and what could, and should, be known. That applies to patients and practitioners alike.) If the patient's suppressed interests are unknown to the practitioner, he or she will accept the practice as unproblematic. Thus a practitioner might unknowingly send a patient with a heart attack to a hospital that restricts treatment. But even if the practitioner knows that the patient's suppressed interests are threatened, the practitioner may none the less regard the matter as a problem whose pragmatic solution, at that time and in that place, is ethically acceptable. So he or she might send the patient to the hospital anyway.

A patients' oppressed interests are, by definition, known to him or her (or easily would be, were he or she to experience the treatment or care). The practitioner is aware there is a problematic issue or practice (or easily should be aware, from professional journals or patient's requests and complaints). But the practitioner presumably supports the solution or policy in place at the time. That support may be from conviction or from necessity. Opposition may put career prospects at risk. Pressure from seniors, managers or peers may be heavy. It is difficult for even dominant interest-holders to go against dominant interests. So for many practitioners, especially junior ones, to open up suppressed and oppressed interests to discussion with the patient is next to impossible.

Then even the discussion of issues where interests are apparently synergistic can throw up conflict. Patients want to be treated to the best of practitioners' ability, and practitioners want to treat them that way. But a patient may ask for something that the practitioner thinks unnecessary or harmful. So there are dilemmas. Real dialogue between patient and practitioner is only feasible when the patient is able to contribute his or her knowledge, perceptions and preferences. There are some professional–consumer encounters where that condition is met. It is met for pregnant women and people with long-term disabilities or chronic illnesses. It is met for people having terminal care at home or in a hospice. So it is unsurprising that pressure groups for these consumers are often concerned with issues of clinical care in its strict sense. It is also unsurprising that once consumers have information about the nature, risks and benefits of various clinical practices, they tend to want to make clinical decisions themselves. This, many professionals find hard to take; for those decisions will not always be in the consumer's best interests, as the practitioner sees them.

Collective clinical care

Consumers' autonomy is at risk a second way when treatment and care move outside the individual clinical relationship into collective clinical care and into non-clinical care.

Collective clinical care is treatment or care outside the individually agreed implicit or explicit contract between practitioner and patient.[8] It generally takes the form of routine treatment or clinical care that professionals assume consumers agree to as a package, without the need for discussion of each bit of string or piece of wrapping paper. Routine antenatal tests, staged over the months of pregnancy at set intervals, are an example. The use of one particular premedication for all patients about to undergo surgery, or the use of one particular sterile solution (or none) for dressing wounds are others. Protocols make for patients' safety when treatment is given by junior or inexperienced staff. So shortages of time and too few practitioners with the right level of skill and judgement can lead to the routinization of treatment and care. But so can practitioners' wish for predictability in their working environment or their personal preferences for particular styles of practice or modes of treatment. Consumerists have the problem here of trying to distinguish accurately between the constraints imposed by lack of resources and the limitations encouraged by staff's self-interest. In the first case, consumers' interests are synergistic with practitioners' – both want more resources put into the clinical activity. In the second case, staff's interests are non-synergistic with consumers'.

Collective clinical care is not protected by clinical freedom. It cannot be, because it derives no authority from agreement between individual practitioner and patient. But the boundary between it and clinical care in the strict sense is often uncertain. That makes it difficult for outsiders to comment on.

Non-clinical care

Non-clinical care means care outside the clinical relationship. It applies to the environmental aspects of clinical settings; to organizational routines that are not part of diagnosis or treatment, and to interactions and communications between practitioners and non-clinical staff (like porters, receptionists or cleaners) that are not part of individual or collective clinical care. Many non-clinical aspects of care threaten consumers' autonomy and interests severely, simply because they are so little open to negotiation between practitioner and patient. On the other hand, because they are not subject to the protection of clinical freedom, it is easy for members of consumer groups to ask questions about them and comment on them. And it is relatively easy for consumerists to formulate or promote standards for non-clinical care. One of consumerists' strategies has been to redefine clinical matters as non-clinical, so that they could criticize them. They have drawn the meaning of 'clinical' away from 'anything done by a clinician or in a clinical setting' to the narrower definitions given above. But in reality there are overlaps between clinical care in its strict or narrow sense and wide sense, and between clinical and non-clinical care.

Autonomy

Consumers' autonomy has a threefold importance to consumer pressure groups: ethical, political and therapeutic.

- The ethical part is a matter of conviction about individuals' moral status and responsibility.
- The political part is linked, for some consumerists, to concerns about the distribution of power in society. Interests in health care are different from the socioeconomic interests of party politics. But the radical element that makes consumerism parallel in some ways to feminism, makes it parallel in others to left-wing political thought and to anti-racism. The common theme is structural disadvantage; disadvantage to consumers, to women, to the working class and to ethnic minorities that is pervasively supported by society's institutions and values. Consumers' autonomy is thus a political (in its widest sense) good to those consumerists.
- The therapeutic part is the most complex. Autonomy means self-determination and the means to it, like information and choice. Consumer pressure groups pick up any evidence that information or choice or control or making decisions can help patients clinically – benefit their responses to sickness, speed their recovery, help them stay well longer. Where that evidence exists, the therapeutic argument then reinforces the ethical and political position. And it is much more persuasive to most dominant interest-holders. It appeals to those of their interests that are almost always synergistic with consumers': their interests in the consumers' clinical welfare. Put another way, it appeals to their ideology about acting in patients' best interests. To the extent that pressure groups can demonstrate that care that supports some aspect of consumers' autonomy, improves clinical outcomes, they can change professional practices and standards. For then most health-care professionals will (in time) alter their practices and standards accordingly.

Standards to do with information, choice or control are among the 'agreed standards' discussed in Chapter 1: standards in which consumers' and professionals' interests become synergistic after the resolution of conflicts over oppressed or suppressed interests. Thus we have moved on from the dynamics of standards to their content, to what they are about.

Consumer pressure groups are little known to people outside them. So some points about their origins, their ideologies, their relations with professionals, and with the government, will form the context for a discussion of the sources of the standards they promote. How near their standards are to those of 'ordinary' consumers is the subject of Chapter 3. Examples will be taken mainly from two pressure groups. The Association for Improvements in the Maternity Services (AIMS) is chiefly concerned with clinical care. It and other maternity care pressure groups have opened up the public discussion of interests and standards in clinical care further than pressure groups in other specialties. The other pressure group, the National Association for the Welfare of Children in Hospital (NAWCH) has led the field in articulating and promoting standards of non-clinical care. Their specialty is paediatrics. Both groups have been to a great extent successful, though they have worked differently. So they illustrate well the conflicts and convergencies between consumerist standards and professional standards, and the translation of one into the other.

ORIGINS OF CONSUMER PRESSURE GROUPS

Consumer pressure groups, like other social organizations, are creatures of their time and place. They arise in reaction to professional and institutional practices. But they only arise when an individual or small group of people discover that their interests in health care, or those of people like them, or of people they care about, are harmed by current practices. Founders of consumer pressure groups may or may not see those practices in terms of interests. People have initially an intuitive rather than an analytic sense of their own interests. So what is experienced is perceived as poor care or low standards, even though the standards may be considered high by the practitioners carrying them out.

It is sometimes supposed that unpleasant experiences of health care prompt people to start consumer pressure groups. But there are more unpleasant experiences than there are pressure groups. The experience has to be one that threatens the self. AIMS was started in 1960, after Sally Willington spent six weeks in an antenatal ward where she experienced the care as cruel.[9] That was a direct affront to the self. But trigger experiences can also be vicarious, through identification. Identification, feeling in imagination what another sentient being must feel of distress or contentment, is part of our capacity for connectedness to each other and to the natural world. It contributes to the great humane movements of the past and present like anti-slavery and anti-whaling. It is enhanced by circumstances that increase sensitivity to particular predicaments. Thus a group of young mothers, reading about the plight of young children denied their mothers' presence in hospital by policies that curtailed parents' visits to their children to a few hours a day or a week, founded NAWCH in 1961. None had had a child in hospital herself.[10] Similarly, the Patients Association was founded in 1963, when Helen Hodgson heard about research on patients, without their knowledge or consent, and about medical students' examinations of patients, without their prior consent.[11]

Thus consumer pressure groups are started from a vivid sense of the harmfulness of some professional or institutional practices. The harm in the cases of AIMS and NAWCH was to oppressed interests. In the case of the Patients Association it was to suppressed interests.

Ideologies

The strong feelings that are called for in starting a consumer pressure group have to attract support from other people who share or understand those feelings. So the experiences that evoke those feelings have to be common. Pressure groups are started to oppose routine, not rare, practices and standards. Whatever the trigger events and the early responses to it, consumer pressure groups keep going most surely if their members can abstract their passionate concern into one or two essential principles that reflect a coherent theoretical framework. Those principles sustain the morale, or sense of moral purpose, of the group. Consumer groups, like professional ones, need ideologies. Then as circumstances change, and as the first standards a group pressed for are adopted by the health service (or, more rarely, discarded by the group), the group can respond to new issues from that theoretical framework or its implications. A group's position on any new issue will not always be consistent with the theoretical framework; but it usually will. Changing circumstances may lead members to alter somewhat the theoretical framework and the principles it sustains (probably then with some resignations of early members); and so the group will develop with the times.

AIMS and NAWCH were founded within a year of each other, 1960 and 1961. Both were started by mothers of young children. Both set off with advantages. Their members were well and active; energy is needed to oppose dominant interests. Because their members were not sick, old or handicapped, there were no problems of stigma. The members were strongly motivated by their love for their children. And they had a degree of authority by reason of their responsibility for them. The groups came into being at a time when mothers were expected to stay at home to look after their children. Thirty years later, that may seem a facet of women's oppression. But it meant that the founders were highly educated and articulate, and invested a great deal of themselves in their roles as mothers. At the same time, the writings of people like John Bowlby and Donald Winnicott about the mother–child relationship reinforced as well as shaped those mothers' feelings and provided them with arguments to support their cases for changes in professional practice.[12,13]

NAWCH believed that children's emotional development was best safeguarded, especially under the severe stress of being in hospital, by their parents' presence. The underlying theoretical framework was psychoanalytic. It attributed great importance to parents and especially to a 'good enough' mother's intuitive capacity to make both the inner and outer stresses a child meets (that is, both unconscious anxieties and the anxieties that illness and its treatment entail) tolerable to the child.[14] Parents had the right as well as the duty, the wish as well as the capacity, to protect their children and their long-term interests.

NAWCH's most basic standard for the psychosocial care of children in hospital was their unrestricted access to their parents. NAWCH's early work concentrated on trying to secure acceptance of this standard. The principle, the need to safeguard children's emotional development, led on to pressing for parents' unrestricted access to special and intensive care units for new born babies; living-in accommodation for parents; a parent's presence during the induction and recovery from anaesthesia; the provision of substitute mothering for children without a parent in hospital; the further protection of children's emotional and intellectual development in hospital through play under the skilled help of a play worker; parents sharing with nurses the care of the child; appropriate facilities in hospital for adolescents; and parents' rights to full explanations of risks and benefits before they give consent to treatments for their children.[15] NAWCH did not take up strictly clinical issues, though it occasionally drew attention to the need for higher professional standards in, for example, pain control for children. It came instead to an understanding with professionals that they were the experts in the clinical treatment of the child;

NAWCH was the expert on the psychosocial and non-clinical care of the child; and parents were the experts in the care of their own children.[16]

The principle AIMS believed in was choice in childbirth. The theoretical framework underlying that was the proposition that pregnancy and childbirth were primarily socio-physiological events, not primarily medico-pathological ones. Pregnancy and childbirth were not illnesses. No-one yet knew exactly what the most propitious conditions for childbirth were. Pragmatically as well as ethically, women must make their own choices about their labour and the care of their newborn babies. Those choices should be made in the light of accurate information about the risks and benefits of various courses of action, as far as they are known, and with advice and support from their doctors and midwives.

Defining pregnancy and childbirth as non-medical meant that their every aspect could come under AIMS' scrutiny and comment. AIMS felt no hesitation in studying and commenting on clinical matters. It believed that all pregnant and labouring women should, if they wished, take up the option, implicit in the clinical relationship, of querying every aspect of their treatment and care. They also believed that self-determination and autonomy meant that women's decisions should prevail over professional decisions in cases of irreconcilable conflict. (Saying that AIMS' definition of pregnancy and childbirth let them scrutinize clinical matters may seem to contradict the earlier point that it is consumers' ability to contribute to discussion that enables them and their professional advisors to use the strict clinical relationship to explore the consumers' interests fully. But both are true. People with long-term conditions tend to redefine them as normal, though limiting, rather than as states of sickness.[17] They also tend to be dissatisfied with varying and inconsistent clinical advice and to build up their own expertise in the management of their condition.)[18]

The first choices for which AIMS campaigned were for each woman's choice of whether to have the baby's father with her throughout labour and birth (fathers were excluded then for part or all of labour) and for choice of place of birth (hospital or home). Choice thereafter has continued to be fastened back into the definition of childbirth as a normal physiological process. So AIMS has scrutinized each new obstetric technology as it has been introduced and has tried to protect women's right to refuse (or ask for) any intervention in the course of pregnancy or labour. It has

resisted creeping routinization of technology's use, when interventions come to be taken so much for granted by staff that they
omit to discuss each with each woman, and to gain her consent or
refusal. The issues it has taken up include the routine use of foetal
monitoring; of induction of labour; of shaving pubic hair; of
enemas; of antenatal ultrasound; of Syntometrine toward the end of
labour; and of the rising rate of caesarian sections.[19] It has also
worked for parents' decisions about non-clinical matters, like how
to feed and care for their babies, to be respected.

As well as pressing for standards that make explicit and safeguard
choice of treatment, AIMS has constantly criticized the treatments
('interventions') themselves. It believes that obstetrics is not a
scientifically-based specialty. It thinks that obstetricians adopt new
clinical practices without insisting on evidence of their safety or
understanding of their consequential effects on the course of
labour.[20] In saying this, AIMS is only saying what many people,
professional and lay, would take for granted about the whole of
medical, nursing and paramedical knowledge and practice. None of
these is an exact science; and even if they were, sciences themselves
are shaped and limited by their time and place. More significant
therefore is AIMS' accusation that obstetricians (and midwives) fail
to evaluate research and their own practices properly. That this is so
in all specialties, is also a common view, expressed in medical,
nursing and health economics journals. AIMS, however, is among
the few consumer pressure groups that persistently declare it, and
cite evidence in its support. (The National Childbirth Trust (NCT)
and MIND, the National Association for Mental Health, have also
criticized specific treatments and clinical practices.) But it is AIMS'
view that women should insist on being treated as responsible adults
capable of making decisions about their own care and that of their
foetuses that has perhaps been the greatest challenge to dominant
interests. It has prompted dominant interest-holders to redefine the
foetus as a patient separate from the mother, whose views may
conflict with its welfare and can therefore be overridden.[21]

Relations with professionals

NAWCH's exclusion of clinical care from its remit, and AIMS'
inclusion of it, affects their relationships with professionals. One of
the most important strategic decisions consumer pressure groups
have to take is about that relationship. Members of consumer

pressure groups, and individual consumerists, tend to feel anger towards professionals in general, just as professionals tend to feel antagonism towards them. Issues to do with standards raise strong feelings and stir conflicts beneath the surface of things. Fundamental interests are at stake, not only in autonomy, but also in how life shall be lived and sickness and disability surmounted. But most consumer pressure groups choose to form alliances with individual professionals whom they perceive as 'good'. (A 'good' professional is a proto-professional; one who works to make professional interests in an issue or practice synergistic with consumers' suppressed or oppressed interests.) Towards these 'good' professionals hostility is replaced by esteem. An amicable relationship suits the pressure group. 'Good' professionals can give advice; tell consumer groups about aspects of care of which they knew nothing (it is often professionals who disclose suppressed interests); and help them interpret technical data. Moreover, it is only practising professionals who can try out new ways of doing things and derive new ideas and standards from that experience. Again, it is professionals who can most easily put new standards into practice in the wards or departments in which they work. (In the last few years, professionals have begun to take the view that all standards must be 'owned' by them; that none can be 'imposed' by managers or professionals higher in organizational hierarchies. This is a change from the days when decisions about standards lay with consultants and ward sisters or charge nurses in hospitals, and GPs and sisters in the community.[22] It is a threat to consumerist standards in some ways, though it recognizes that standards introduced by senior staff were often disregarded by junior staff.) Lastly, since the 'credibility' of professionals is higher with their peers than consumerists' credibility, professionals have more chance of influencing those peers' practice. So many new consumer pressure groups invite 'good' professionals to help them.

Reciprocally, an amicable relationship suits those professionals. It gives them access to the consumer group's expertise and networks. It gives them support in their own attempts to introduce new standards. It gives them a platform, literally at conferences, metaphorically in consumerists' journals. It can give them the high profile that is fame. But associating with a consumer group that is too radical can harm professionals' reputation amongst their peers. Thus NAWCH has the goodwill of many paediatricians and paediatric nurses largely because it does not take up positions on clinical matters. AIMS, by contrast, has the goodwill of fewer obstetricians and midwives, apart from the Association of Radical Midwives, itself a break-away group from mainstream midwifery.

The NAWCH national executive committee has paediatricians and paediatric nurses on it, as well as parents. The AIMS committee is drawn from parents only. NAWCH, through stressing synergistic interests and good relationships, can use professionals to make comments in public that it could make for itself.

■ NAWCH used a consultant paediatrician, a paediatric nurse advisor, an Ear, Nose and Throat (ENT) ward sister and an ENT surgeon to criticize a leaflet produced by an ENT surgeon for parents of children about to undergo surgery. The locality and the names were not given.[23]

Then, too, friendly cooperation, even with 'good' professionals, depends on refraining from attacking the other camp's regular soldiers. NAWCH is careful not to name in public 'bad' hospitals and 'bad' paediatricians. AIMS uses emphatic language and identifies 'bad' professionals with derision.

■ Over the last few years the AIMS committee has become increasingly concerned by the numbers of women and babies also who have been assaulted during childbirth and afterwards: women who have been given treatment and procedures against their wishes [in English law this constitutes assault except under defined circumstances]; babies who have been removed to the SCBU [Special Care Baby Unit or nursery] against the wishes of the parents; babies who have been given bottled milk, in spite of the parents giving strict instructions that the babies were to be only breastfed. These are just a few examples of the widespread abuse of parents' wishes.[24]

■ Following an argument in which the consultant maintained that the baby's head was engaged [i.e. in the pelvis, so that the baby would be born head-first] and the mother considered that the baby was breech, the consultant terminated the matter with the following statement: 'There is not a woman on this earth who can tell me anything about being pregnant.' Mr [named], Consultant Obstetrician [named hospital]. *Note* – The woman subsequently gave birth to [the] baby in the breech position.[25]

These differences in relationships, connected as they are to remit and ideology, make differences to the extent to which pressure groups' standards are accepted and promoted by the Department of Health.

Relations with government

The power either to recommend specific standards of care, as guidance, or to enforce them by statute, or to do nothing, lies with government. This power partly derives from government's general duty to safeguard citizens' welfare. But it also derives in this country from the status of the NHS as a public service, for which the Secretary of State at the Department of Health is accountable to parliament. Most professional interest groups and most consumer pressure groups seek to keep in contact with the Department and hope to influence it.

Government as an abstraction, and civil servants in the Department of Health in their persons, can be called corporate rationalizers. With managers in local health services, public health doctors, and some academic clinicians and clinical research workers, they make up the third group of interest-holders in the health service.[26,27] Their interests are called challenging because from time to time they challenge dominant interests. The changes in the organization of the NHS, introduced by a Conservative Government in 1991, implemented by managers and resisted at first by many health-care professionals (and some consumerists), is an example of such a challenge.

Corporate rationalizers' interests are to do with the rational use of resources. The changes just mentioned were intended to secure a better use of resources. Practitioners and patients think of health care at the level of individuals. Corporate rationalizers think of it at the level of populations. So they want to see efficient and effective care for populations rather than individuals. (An individual's and a population's interests may or may not be synergistic here. The successful control of infectious disease usually benefits both. Keeping alive very premature sick babies may benefit neither.) Corporate rationalizers, health-care professionals and consumers can be thought of as the three apices of a triangle. Each's interests can be synergistic with either or both of the other's. Or they can be non-synergistic with either or both. Figure 2.1 shows this triangle. Again, as with dominant and repressed interests, challenging interests are not inevitably tied to the corresponding interest-holders.

Corporate rationalizers support repressed interests and re-pressed interest-holders by helping consumer pressure groups. The Department gives grants to some groups for organizational

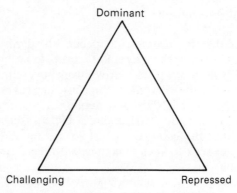

Figure 2.1 Synergies and non-synergies between dominant, challenging and repressed interests.

expenses or research. It consults with consumer groups. It sometimes agrees to put specific standards about treatment and care into guidance for health authorities, or to make them compulsory. Consumerists always want to see at least minimum standards made compulsory: professionals always want to retain discretion, the gentle word for power.

Now the word challenge means to call into question, to summon to a contest.[28] It comes from the Latin *calumnia*, trickery, perhaps because winning contests often requires guile as well as power. Government ministers, civil servants in the Department of Health and local managers are high in rhetoric about putting patients first.[29] But at the end of the day (to use a favourite phrase of managers that reflects their sense of the vicissitudes of battle), corporate rationalizers usually support dominant interests against oppressed or suppressed interests. (If they did not, health professionals' interests could not sustain their dominance, because government is more powerful than health professionals.) The extent to which corporate rationalizers support any consumer pressure group and its desired standards depends largely on the extent to which leading professionals support them. (Leading professionals are professionals with credibility amongst their peers. They may or may not be proto-professionals.) When leading professionals oppose consumer groups' standards, corporate rationalizers tend to feel that siding with repressed interests would entail too much trouble. Or it would involve too high a risk of jeopardizing more important issues on corporate rationalizers' agendas.

Thus NAWCH receives an annual grant from the Department. (In 1989 it was £93 550.)[30] AIMS receives nothing.[31] NAWCH's standards have been promoted in government guidance for the last 30 years (Chapter 6). AIMS' standards have not. NAWCH is in touch with the Department of Health. AIMS has not been invited there in recent years.[32] It would be too simple to suppose that the difference depends entirely on differences in ideology and in relationships with dominant interest-holders. For one thing, NAWCH is the only consumer pressure group working for its kind of standards in paediatric care. Several other maternity pressure groups have views and promote standards that overlap with AIMS', though AIMS is the only group solely concerned with maternity care. That makes it difficult to attribute standards promoted by the Department to one group or another. But the general observation that corporate rationalizers only accept consumerist standards to the extent that leading professionals do is borne out.

Sources of standards

Standards are ideas. Ideas can come from anywhere. Every new idea and standard of a consumerist sort starts from a breakdown of the consensual view of the health service. Differences in interests become apparent, replacing the view that they were synergistic, when discrepancies develop between health professionals' knowledge and sensibility and knowledge and sensibility amongst the wider population. There are various sorts of disjunction: gaps in professional knowledge; the maintainance of technically outmoded practices; the introduction of new practices incongruent with changing ethical or moral values; or the development of different perceptions and assumptions between professionals and consumers or consumerists.

The issues that consumer pressure groups pick up and pursue come from their members' experience and observation. They come from letters and telephone calls from constituents (members of the care group). They also come from health-care professionals who are uneasy about what they see in their work. Lastly, but importantly, they come from professionals and academics in other disciplines. At the same time, proto-professionals pick up these issues, too, and work within their own networks, or with consumerists. It is therefore usually difficult to identify the precise sources of a consumerist standard.

It happens that NAWCH's and AIMS' first standards can be identified. They illustrate how quickly consumerist and professional sources of ideas can overlap, consumer groups picking up proto-professional standards, and professional groups advocating consumerist standards.

Thus NAWCH's object when it was founded was to secure the implementation of the Platt Report, *The Welfare of Children in Hospital* (1959). This report came into being after James and Joyce Robertson had shown how serious was the suffering of young children in hospital. Written under the chairmanship of the President of the Royal College of Surgeons, the report had 51 recommendations elaborating the first general one:[33]

> Greater attention needs to be paid to the emotional and mental [psychological] needs of the child in hospital, against the background of changes in attitudes towards children, in the hospital's place in the community, and in medical and surgical practice. The authority and responsibility of parents, the individuality of the child, and the importance of mitigating the effects of the break with home should all be more fully recognised.

Those recommendations were cast in the form of standards, most of which NAWCH adopted at first, though it extended and refined many of them later.

AIMS' first standard was that women should be given the choice of having the father of their child with them at any stage of labour.[34] It preceded the enunciation of a cautious form of that standard a few months later in the Ministry of Health's *Human Relations in Obstetrics*, 1961:[35]

> . . . it should be possible to allow the husband to visit as frequently as he is able [in the first stage of labour] providing, of course, that there is nothing in the patient's condition to contra-indicate it and both partners desire it. . . . In any case the mother's own wish must be consulted. Whether the patient's husband stays during the second stage [the birth] depends on the individual circumstances of each case.

These examples illustrate the dynamic interplay of interests, feelings and ideas that create a new consumerist standard. Interests, feelings and ideas lead to new professional and proto-professional standards, too. But professionals often (indeed, usually) formulate standards without referring them to consumers or consumerists, or consulting them.[36] Consumerists are always aware of professionals. Consumerists are always mindful of the need for negotiation or for pressure, for redefinition of the familiar or for new evidence, to get their standards accepted. Repressed interest-holders and those who speak for them have to study dominant interest-holders more carefully than the other way about.[37] That is another of the paradoxes of professionalism and consumerism.

CONSUMERISTS' AND CONSUMERS' STANDARDS

. . . the aim of a life can only be to increase the sum of freedom and responsibility to be found in every [person] and in the world. It cannot, under any circumstances, be to reduce or suppress that freedom, even temporarily.

Albert Camus (1961)[1]

INTRODUCTION

How close are consumerists' standards to those of 'ordinary' consumers? How accurately do consumerists identify 'ordinary' consumers' interests? Consumerists want to believe they speak for them. Some dominant interest-holders hope they do not. Some corporate rationalizers seem to think that there is a population of naive consumers who subscribe to neither professional nor consumerist standards, but to a third, authentic, set, if only what that is could be discovered.

Four lines of argument and evidence point to the answer: the nature of consumerist standards; research into consumers' views; the views of groups of users convened by health authorities or other statutory bodies; and consumers' narrative accounts of their health care.

THE NATURE OF CONSUMERIST STANDARDS

Most consumer pressure groups promote two kinds of standards. The first is directed towards widening consumers' choices and supporting their autonomy; I shall call them 'general core standards'. The second are standards that the group thinks right for consumers' care and treatment; they can be called 'specialty-specific' or 'specialist standards'. The two kinds are often combined or implied in a single statement. Thus the NAWCH standard for the visiting of children in hospital, unrestricted access by children to their parents, upholds parents' freedom to be with their child (and the reciprocal, children's right to have their parents' presence), in order that parents can support and protect their children in hospital. In order that parents can do this, they must have freedom of access to their children.

General core standards seek to secure wider options for consumers rather than narrower ones; they are liberating rather than restricting.[2] That follows from their history. Many are articulated and promoted in revolt against professional and institutional policies and practices. They move in the direction of restraining restrictions over consumers. This can be seen from the stages through which consumerist standards progress. NAWCH's first definition of 'unrestricted' visiting meant long daily visiting hours for parents, in place of an hour or less on some days, and none on others, common in hospitals in the early 1960s. The definition of unrestricted (i.e. the value attached to the standard) moved to 24 hours a few years later. That is the highest quantitative standard possible.

So general core standards promote things like:

● minimum constraints over in-patients' access to visitors or over out-patients bringing companions to consultations;
● maximum access to information, for those who wish to have it, about, for example, their condition and what options there are for treating it;
● maximum choices of all kinds, major and minor – e.g. of date for admission for elective surgery, of menu, of whether to get up for breakfast or stay in bed – for those choices which help consumers to manage their health care as seems best to them.

The greater the freedom for consumers that a standard secures, the higher the standard. That is how consumerists tell higher from lower.

Specialty-specific or specialist standards start from general core standards because it is usually consumers' wish to safeguard their interests in some specific way that leads them to promote autonomy and choice. The development of expertise is the next step. Effective consumer pressure groups know that pressing for the adoption of their standards calls for a convincing case. Its components have to come from sources and in a language that professionals understand. Consumer groups have to study professional journals in order to challenge professionals on their ground. Professional journals regularly contain papers and articles about deficiencies in treatment and care or about new ways of doing things. A great deal of consumerist work can be done from those sources.[3]

Established consumer pressure groups also pay close attention to research in disciplines apart from medicine and nursing. Ethological, sociological and psychological papers are scanned. The range reflects consumer groups' search for evidence, however eclectic, to support their views. Professionals are expected to read thoroughly within their specialities. But they seldom have reason to search beyond them. Dominant interest-holders can float in the mainstream of knowledge about their speciality: repressed interest-holders have to paddle up the sidestreams to find what they need.

As well as theoretical knowledge, many consumer groups have a comprehensive picture of the range of professional practices and institutional policies. They hear of differing practices from their members or constituents. That variation, in part the result of professionals' freedom to fall short of the accepted standards of the day, as well as to rise above them, is important to consumer pressure groups. It enables them to demonstrate the feasibility of the standards they desire.

Thus consumer pressure groups develop a specialist knowledge of some aspects of treatment and care, though it is different from professionals' knowledge. Guided by their ideologies, they come to favour some clinical and non-clinical approaches more than others. A few they condemn. This applies most commonly to non-clinical care. But consumer pressure groups concerned with clinical care hold strong views about it. Thus some mental health pressure groups, like Survivors Speak Out and the London Alliance for Mental Health Action, are opposed to psychotropic medication or to ECT (electroconvulsive therapy) for anyone with mental illness.[4] Others, like the Schizophrenia Association of Great Britain, believe that these drugs are nearly always beneficial if correctly prescribed, though they think that they are very often prescribed unskilfully.[5] Whatever their slant, consumer groups articulate specialist standards based on their knowledge and their values.

The distinction between general core standards and specialist standards helps answer the question at the beginning of this chapter. General core standards expand the possibilities open to consumers. They support whatever wish they have to take advantage of those possibilities. So they are likely to accord with the standards consumers would choose for themselves. Specialist standards are problematic. Since they do not always match each other in different consumer groups for the same speciality, that must be so. In that, they are exactly parallel to professional standards and their variations.

■ Margaret K. Nelson interviewed women in Vermont, USA in a hospital whose stated policy was that women could choose their style of birth. She categorized her sample of 226 women into two social classes. Before their babies' births, middle-class women wanted to have active births, with little obstetric intervention. Working-class women preferred passive births, with more monitoring, medication and use of forceps. (The one wanted to enjoy the births, the other to get them over quickly.) So again, the general core standard of choice was important to both groups. But their choices of standards for clinical care were different. However, neither group's preferences were fully respected by staff. They favoured and implemented an approach of their own.[6] So both groups of women failed to receive what they wanted.

Although consumerist specialist standards are problematic, they immediately appeal to some consumers' perceptions of their interests. As a truism, standards gain currency through their spread and spread because they gain currency. The media publish some of them. (Women's magazines play a part here, especially for standards for women's and children's health care.) 'Ordinary' consumers hear of them. In the Vermont study, working-class women's preferences for style of birth were closer to middle-class preferences if the working class women had read about childbirth or attended classes in preparation for it.[7] After a time, consumerist specialist standards begin to be adopted by proto-professionals, and then by some 'ordinary' professionals. Once new specialist standards have begun to be put into practice, some consumers adopt or expect them, simply because they are familiar.[8] In addition, the surveys used to ascertain the views and preferences of 'ordinary' consumers tend to be based on questionnaires first devised by consumer pressure groups. Thus many CHCs, charged with finding out what consumers think of local services, adapt national consumer pressure groups' questionnaires. (It is relatively easy to modify other people's questionnaires. It is difficult to invent an entirely new one.) So the range of issues chosen and some of the questions asked are repeated. In that way, CHCs' own views, and the views of the 'ordinary' consumers whose perceptions are sought, are shaped and constrained by the instruments used. It is perhaps ironic that professionals' reluctance to solicit consumers' views of professional practice has left the field so open for consumerists to occupy.

Thus it happens that many consumers will gradually move towards wanting or willingly accepting consumerist specialist standards, through the social processes that influence knowledge and sensibility. Some consumers move further than others. There will seldom be complete uniformity in either what is offered or what is wanted. Consumerist specialist standards keep debate about different patterns of care and treatment alive. Consumerist general standards affirm the importance of choice in that diversity.

RESEARCH INTO CONSUMERS' VIEWS

Direct and systematic research into consumers' standards is scant. Few people have reason to undertake it. Professionals usually believe that the standards they work to are the best, or at any rate the best under the circumstances. They imagine consumers' standards to be low and so irrelevant. (Consumers' expectations sometimes are low, especially when their interests are suppressed. Consumers can hardly expect to benefit from something of whose existence they know nothing. That can make their views seem pitifully simple to staff, who do know.) Conversely, professionals fear that consumers' standards will be too high, and so demand more time or effort or clinical resources than can be given easily.

In parallel, consumerists often believe that they know what consumers' standards are. But they are nervous lest those should turn out to be lower than the ones they advocate, exposing the consumerists as extremists. Or they fear that consumers' standards will be higher than those they advocate, undermining their claim to represent consumers' views.

Managers have little to gain by probing, as long as institutions and systems run smoothly.

In addition, direct research into consumers' standards requires setting out the full range of values a standard could have and asking consumers to mark or say their preferences.

Would you like to be addressed by your	first name and surname title and surname don't mind
Should doctors introduce themselves?	very important important not important

(Readers are invited to add the missing values in these examples.[9]) But managers are reluctant to set out full ranges. They fear it would result in inconvenient choices or in raised expectations. Even some academics advise those about to carry out surveys to investigate only issues where changes in policy and practice would be feasible, that is, acceptable to staff. That advice is a powerful support to dominant interests.

It is therefore unsurprising that research into consumers' standards is sparse. There is, however, some work that is suggestive of consumers' standards, albeit only within the range of values offered and under the conditions obtaining at the time of the survey:[10]

■ A three-month period of new visiting hours from 2 p.m. to 8 p.m., instead of two shorter periods, was tried in six acute wards in York District General Hospital, after staff had refused to agree to the longer visiting hours. Patients, visitors and staff were asked their preferences. 88 per cent of 88 patients and 90 per cent of 96 visitors preferred the longer hours. 67 per cent of 46 staff did not. The extended period was brought in to all adult acute wards.

Although direct research into consumers' standards is meagre, there are other sorts of survey from which their standards can be deduced. One is research into consumers' experiences of health care, the other into their satisfaction with it.

Research into consumers' experiences of health care, or satisfaction with it, tell us about their standards, provided that the respondents are invited to make evaluative comments on what they describe, or to describe what they evaluate. Unfortunately these conditions are met erratically. Satisfaction or opinion surveys are especially prone to absurdities like asking if respondents were told 'enough' about something, without either asking what they were told or giving a checklist of what they might have been told. For local small-scale research, omissions can be partly repaired if what happened is known from other sources and is matched (with their permission) to respondents' answers. But omissions cannot be wholly made good because only each respondent knows how he or she perceived what happened.

■ North West Thames RHA commissioned useful research into out-patients' experiences. It showed that they were concerned with what I have called general core standards: things to do with 'being dealt with courteously and as an adult'; with information of all sorts; privacy; the 'manner of medical and nursing staff'; and continuity of care – seeing the same doctor from visit to visit and being recognized by the receptionists.

Consumers' 'elements of good practice' (i.e. standards) for adequacy of information included: 'having information provided in sufficient detail to understand it, expressed with precision and in terms that are intelligible; being given the "full" story – what has happened to date, what is happening now, what is to happen next; and medical staff using illustrations and diagrams to explain points'.[11] That fits with consumerist standards for information, discussed in Chapter 7.

Conspicuously missing from most surveys sponsored by health authorities, CHCs and other organizations are questions about consumers' experiences and opinions of clinical care. That includes both clinical care in the strict sense and collective clinical care. Their omission is another tribute to the power of dominant interests, a tribute often paid before it has been sought. The taboo is so strong that in the work by North West Thames RHA, interviewers were instructed to not to write down any spontaneous comments that respondents might make about individual members of staff or about clinical care.[12] That was throwing away data about respondents' concerns and perceptions. In that, it failed to respect respondents. Moreover, it destroyed the chance of discovering what consumers valued in their clinical care quite as much as it suppressed their views of what was bad.

The most notable exception to reticence about enquiring into clinical matters is in maternity care. By defining pregnancy and childbirth as non-medical, consumer groups have opened them up to lay scrutiny. By surveying large numbers of their own members, and by inviting through the media other women to write in, the groups have freed themselves from dominant interest-holders' censorship. Such samples are biased towards certain sorts of women. But in showing that there are problems to look into, consumer groups have stimulated further research and discussion:[13]

■ A study of clinical experiences was done by Sheila Kitzinger for the National Childbirth Trust and published in 1975. Mrs Kitzinger used birth reports, accounts written by women who had taken part in NCT classes in preparation for childbirth. In examining 614 reports of induction of labour and 224 of spontaneous labour, she found that many women had disliked induction intensely, though some had liked it. There were grounds for ethical concern about clinical practices. Some women said that induction had been started without their knowledge or consent. The analgesic pethidine, that can suppress newborn babies' breathing reflexes and cause them sucking difficulties, had sometimes been injected in spite of a woman's refusal of it. And there were grounds for concern about clinical practices. Babies had been induced mistakenly early. The severe pain of the contractions resulting from induction had necessitated epidural anaesthesia, with its associated risks of forceps delivery and need for nursing the baby in a special care nursery away from the mother. Inductions had been started and stopped over several days, so that labour only took place in the daytime, an especially distressing and painful experience.

This study began to change both professional and consumers' attitudes to induction. Later studies supported the findings.[14] But those consumers' descriptions and evaluations of their experiences helped bring some of these serious problems with induction to light. The rate of induction dropped from a peak in 1974 of 39.4 per cent to 17.3 per cent in 1984, though the current rate varies between regions.[15]

What can be called consumers' clinical standards came out of such studies. These include that: greater care should be taken in making decisions about what interventions are made in labour; discussion and consent are necessary in obstetrics, as in other specialities; labours in which women experience extra stress because of interventions require extra psychosocial support from midwives.[16]

Those standards were in theory professional standards already. But consumers' views and consumerist pressure had drawn professionals' and managers' attention to their importance. A statement in 1991 by the Royal College of Midwives noted that:[17]

> organizations representing consumers have expressed concern about levels of intervention and it is evident that some women experience routine interventions determined by clinical protocol rather than their needs . . . all interventions whether medical or non-medical should be validated by research and interventions should be justified by the individual woman's needs.

Also in 1991, a set of guidelines from the Welsh Office stipulated that 'rational protocols' with 'careful selection' for interventions were necessary for 'health gain'.[18] Thus convergence of consumers' and professional standards appears to be taking place over these clinical matters.

There are few technical or clinical procedures in medicine, nursing and paramedical activities that are without immediate, short-term or long-term effects on consumers. Finding out what consumers feel and think is important both in itself and as a potential contribution to higher professional standards.[19] What the work in maternity care shows is that asking consumers questions begins to enable them to frame answers. Repressed interest-holders can understand technical terms, if explanation is offered. But that understanding does not necessarily convert them to an unquestioning acceptance of professional assumptions and values. Rather, it may open up suppressed or oppressed interests and start the processes that lead to new synergistic standards.[20]

THE VIEWS OF GROUPS OF USERS

Some managers or practitioners have convened groups of users (consumers or carers) to discuss the local services. Patients Participation Groups were started in some general practices in 1972 and Patients' Councils in psychiatric hospitals in 1986.[21,22] A few health authorities are now setting up user groups in various specialities in order to get 'user input' into their specifications for purchasing or providing services. And there have been *ad hoc* consultations with users from time to time in some authorities.

A user group convened by professionals or managers is likely to accept implicit restrictions to its agenda. It is easiest for many users to talk about provision and general matters. It is easiest for managers and professionals to listen to them when they do. Patient Participation Groups discuss such matters as the desirability of a woman partner in an all man practice; privacy; ramps; parking; surgery hours and appointment systems; preventive and screening programmes; and home visiting for the elderly.[23] Patients' Councils discuss things like improving signposting in a hospital; having more games and magazines in the patients' lounge; funding for murals in corridors and wards; complaints about inadequate heating and about waiting time to see a doctor; information for patients; and plans for hospital closure.[24] These are important issues, both practically and symbolically. It is possible, however, that more sensitive issues, to do with clinical care and consumers' rights, can only be discussed comfortably by groups away from the hospital or the general practitioners' surgery:[25]

■ A group of 15 users of the mental health services (patients and carers) was convened by Newcastle Health Authority to suggest what standards should be incorporated into specifications for purchasing the services. The group suggested the standard that all patients should have their own toothbrushes, underwear and outer clothing. Without the users' identification of those lacks, the purchasing authority would have assumed that such a basic standard did not need specification.

That standard is indeed basic. It has applied to all mental illness hospitals for at least 15 years.[26] Users' groups may have a unique potential for formulating new standards for care and treatment. But so far, they seem mainly to be picking up failures by managers to implement non-controversial standards for provision and the environment of care.

CONSUMERS' NARRATIVES

Consumers' narratives are a rich source of description combined with evaluation. They are regularly published in nursing, medical and consumers' journals. The narrators write to capture the thankfulness, anxiety or anger they felt. They write to manage their experiences by making sense of them. They write to influence policy and practice. Then the criteria by which the writer judges standards become explicit or so strongly implied as to be all but explicit. Many narratives are written with a clarity and force that enables them to communicate another's selfhood and predicament so intensely that the reader's understanding and sympathies are changed. Familiar but tolerated aspects of health care, put into words with passion, gain new urgency. Unfamiliar aspects, put into words with insight, extend our knowledge and enlarge our sensibility. The accounts increase the store of reality available to us.

Important points emerge from such narratives:

1 The writers discuss, often in detail, clinical treatment and care. They take it for granted that clinical matters are central to their experiences and to the purposes of health care.

2 They judge what happens by its helpfulness to them, to their relatives, or to other consumers.

3 The writers seldom make general evaluations of the sort often asked for in patient satisfaction surveys. What is described is specific and particular. So food is not depicted as good or bad. Rather a writer describes being forced to eat a plate of cold porridge; or how one elderly patient coaxed another into eating by making the serving smaller and more appetizing; or the tyrannical futility of giving unpalatable diabetic diets in hospital to people who control their own carbohydrate intake outside it.

4 The writers predominantly judge care and treatment by 'ordinary' criteria, drawn from the common (or ethnic) culture. That this must be so is obvious. But it means that some of the things that practitioners believe are adaptations to the needs of the sick are judged by them as indignities or hardships.

■ ' "Please" and "thank you" are demanded of the elderly, just like children. It grieved me to hear an 86-year old woman, who was desperately ill and who died within a week, being told she had left out a word. "Say please, Mrs. . . ." ' The writer, too, was upbraided, 'A little more courtesy is needed – say thank you nurse'.

Elderly woman in hospital for major surgery (1986)[27]

■ 'Over the years I have been nursed in many hospitals by countless staff and the hardest thing to bear is patronisation and condescension. Phrases such as, "be a good girl", "you're not trying", and "why are we crying?" . . .'

Young woman with rheumatoid arthritis (1985)[28]

The processes of professionalization draw practitioners away from lay assumptions, perceptions and norms and substitute professional ones. The experience has been likened to going through a mirror and seeing the world from the other side.[29] But practitioner and patient still look at each other – a mirror is a glass for looking, a looking glass. Professional norms that deny consumers what they say they need are judged with anguish or anger.

■ 'I am still angry with those doctors who took it on themselves to protect and patronise me with evasive replies to difficult questions. I have learnt something that my doctors find difficult to understand.

The anxiety of uncertainty and the constant churning through a multitude of possibilities are much harder to bear than dealing with bad news and a much more limited range of probabilities. I have found that hope is much easier to maintain when it does not have to cover the whole spectrum from complete cure to imminent death.'

Woman with late stage cancer (1989)[30]

5 There is a theoretical distinction (though the narrators only occasionally make it) between professional standards that consumers find unhelpful and plain poor care or bad behaviour. The same is true for care to ordinary professional standards and outstanding helpful behaviour. These distinctions need to be captured in the planning and analysis of research, if we are to be sure we understand consumers' standards.

■ 'I have lost track of the number of times I have actually been lifted by my broken arm.'

Woman in hospital after a road accident (1989)[31]

6 Though all writers use 'ordinary' criteria to judge things, some use, as well, expert criteria drawn from their own experiences or from consumerist specialist standards. Others, usually health-care professionals, draw on expert criteria from their professional experience or training.

■ 'We had to report to the accident and emergency department [of a specialized paediatric hospital] for the initial assessment [of their nine-week-old baby with a chest infection]. The clerkess was not impressed by my medical title and declined my diagnosis of chest infection, telling me that the doctor would decide. The attendant nursing staff were also not impressed by the obvious respiratory distress of my child and we had to sit and wait for half an hour before achieving the first hurdle of getting into an examination cubicle. This was particularly poignant because as soon as we had made the decision that hospital admission was required we had rushed to the casualty department as fast as possible.'

Father, GP (1988)[32]

■ 'The memory of the staff midwife who, while dealing with hourly respiratory recordings, numerous intravenous lines, and regular blood glucose estimations, still found time to swab our daughter's

fragile skin with evening primrose oil will never fade. It did not
improve the baby's blood gases but it helped us.'

Father, Senior Registrar (1989)[33]

7 Health-care professionals' narratives show that when they or
their relatives have to receive health care, professionals respond
to it in the same ways as lay people. They feel the same surprise,
anger or admiration. Some part of the professional role seems to
be scraped off, as if by jagged glass, as the practitioner goes back
through the mirror. Care is judged by ordinary and expert
criteria, but no longer from the other side of the looking glass.

This discovery or recovery of lay responses to health care can
be painful. Everyone who has a significant experience gains
insight into it; part of the new understanding professionals
describe is the same as any novice consumer's. But some
professionals look back on their own attitudes and practices; on
their ignorance of the institutional customs and routines that did
not affect them in their work; and on the easy rhetoric of
dedication and caring. They feel regret. They sometimes feel
guilt. They resolve to be more sensitive.

■ 'I have never forgotten the midwife who, during a group discussion,
announced that, in her considered opinion, post-natal depression was
something invented by middle-class women who read too many books
and did not have enough to do. That midwife was me.'

Midwife after treatment for post-natal depression[34]

■ 'The most enduring and painful lesson was gained . . . [when] during
one hallucination, I was sedated with chlorpromazine intramuscu-
larly. I would now hesitate to give this drug in this way. It is
excruciatingly painful whereas haloperidol is equally effective and
painless. . . . As doctors I think we also fail to recognize the yoke of
long-term drug treatment. True, for patients it can literally be a
modus vivendi. It can also be a reminder of difficult times and the
generator of inconvenient and disabling side effects. I find that [the
side effects] caused by lithium can be awkward. It is sufficient to give
me sympathy with patients who fail to comply, whether because of
side effects, the implicit dependency of drug treatments, or other
reasons.'

Doctor, after treatment for manic depressive psychosis (1990)[35]

Sometimes professionals who have experienced health care as
patients or relatives take their insights further and become
proto-professionals.

CONCLUSIONS

From these lines of evidence, we can come to two conclusions. The general core standards articulated by consumerists are those many consumers prefer. Some surveys, like that in York District General Hospital, show this by large majorities. Majorities are useful as political counters. But consumerist core standards maximize freedoms for those who choose to take advantage of them, without forcing them on other consumers. From the perspective of individual care, both those freedoms are what matters.

We know little about most consumers' preferences among consumerist specialist standards. But that little points to the need to keep, or develop, variety amongst patterns of care and treatment. Choices of care and treatment should remain open to individuals. What a consumer is offered should not depend upon accidents of geography or of practitioner. And whatever the treatment, it should be to a proper standard of competence and care. The belief that consumers cannot judge clinical matters should not be used as a reason for denying them the opportunity and the means to do so.

4

AUTONOMY AND THERAPEUTIC BENEFITS

I wish my life and decisions to depend upon myself . . . I wish to be a
subject, not an object . . .

Isaiah Berlin (1969)[1]

Forty years ago health care could be said to be about dependency.
Consumerism has changed that. Once the idea that professionals do
not always act in patients' best interests had taken hold, autonomy
began to replace dependency as a central, though ambiguous,
concept.

Autonomy comes from a Greek word meaning the self, one's
own, by oneself, self-determining. Complete autonomy scarcely
exists, since people are dependent in various ways upon other
people and their decisions, known and unknown. That interdepen-
dence and connectedness enriches and protects life.[2] But what we
call autonomy is broadly independence and self-determination.

Autonomy in a narrower sense is decision-making. An autonomous decision is one made by the self. It is presumed to be made in
the self's interests, since no one can know what those interests are as
sensitively as the self can. The decision can be made with help or
advice. But it is still the self's. The opposite, allowing or asking
another person to make the decision, is heteronomy. Paradoxically,
heteronomy can be an autonomous choice. Belief in the other's
greater knowledge or expertise; or indifference to the decision; or a
strategic purpose in asking or agreeing that someone else make the
decision, are choices of that sort.

Autonomy's opposite is dependency. It comes from a Latin word
dependere, to hand down. Heteronomy is sometimes called dependence. Relying on other people to do things physically to or for the

body is also called dependence, or physical dependence. Its opposite is independence. The feelings that prompt someone to stay close to another person who he or she thinks is better able to cope with things at times of anxiety is also called dependency. But Bowlby's idea of attachment is better.[3] Loss or pain or stress evoke those feelings. Often the anxiety or distress feel more intense and pervasive than the threat warrants; they seem to join onto memories or become revivals of feelings of helplessness experienced by the self when an infant. Then they are liable to carry with them exaggerated feelings of fear or gratitude, or both, towards whoever gives physical or psychological comfort to the self. They produce the magic element in dependency: the unconscious belief that exact compliance with a doctor's or nurse's wishes will bring cure and disobedience will bring retribution.[4] Knowing that the first is not true, though the second sometimes is, is one of the pains that autonomous self has to bear. Disease and death cannot be placated.

Heteronomy, physical dependence and attachment also work together and reinforce each other. So physically dependent people, who can use specialized equipment to do things for them, may retain their autonomy more easily than those who must rely on other people. And recovery from temporary weakness helps reduce anxiety and diminishes sensitivity to the nuances of what other people say or do.

The way people experience a sense of autonomy depends upon interacting variables to do with personality, situation, social and cultural factors. But it is regarded as precious in our western society.

Sickness or accident of any but trivial and self-limiting kinds change that; they dissolve the presumption of autonomy. The autonomous self is threatened because it becomes poignantly aware of its own fragility and mortality. Physical energy may be drained. Psychological energy may be swamped by anxiety. The self experiences a dependency on others that it may not wish to feel. Or it may relish dependency but believe it cannot be met by others. It is threatened because if it has to turn for help to health professionals, it generally has to do so on their terms, not its own.

But although people's autonomy in the wide sense of being able to function as an active agent is reduced by sickness or accident, their ability to take decisions about themselves is not necessarily impaired. (Provided they are not unconscious or demented.) Rather, the preoccupation with the self that goes with concern or anxiety may enhance it. Certainly there are new calls upon it. People who are sick (or think they may be) have management tasks and decisions. They have to weigh up the benefits and costs of consulting a doctor. If serious disease is diagnosed, they have to manage their own feelings and thoughts under that threat. They have to manage how they disclose of their predicament to family, friends and colleagues. They have to manage the health professionals round them. (That is difficult without practice, as observations in hospital wards and the transcripts of recorded consultations show. Chapter 7 and Chapter 10 on control and decision-making give examples.) They have to manage those aspects of their sickness, condition or predicament that are not directly managed by practitioners. For many of these management tasks, they have to choose between autonomous or heteronomous decision-making. That in itself is a series of autonomous decisions.

When someone feels that he or she has managed those tasks well, and has been supported rather than undermined in that management, the sickness or predicament can be in a sense transcended.[5] That can be so even if the outcome not good. But if things have gone badly, disappointment or anger can long outlast recovery. Though few people would choose to repeat the terror and risks of serious sickness to perfect their management of themselves and the practitioners round them, there are milder exceptions. When the management of childbirth has been unsatisfactory, some women avoid having another baby. But others resolve to start again with a new pregnancy, to redeem the experience.

PROFESSIONALS AND CONSUMERS

The terms on which professionals help people may or may not be conducive to the successful carrying out of the latters' management tasks. Those terms are shaped by practitioners' management tasks. Practitioners have to manage their feelings and thoughts; their work for and on patients; and their work in the health service. They too have to manage autonomy and heteronomy: making decisions for or about patients, asking them to make their own, or sharing the discussion with them. A new term, 'collaborative autonomy', has come in to heighten the idea of shared decision-making within the clinical relationship.[6] But collaboration has many points on a balance between practitioner and patient. So the patient's and the practitioner's management tasks weigh sometimes with and sometimes against each other, with varying degrees of success as each judges it.

Practitioners have more opportunities for perfecting their management skills than do patients. But patients' variability and the opacity of their management strategies can be misleading. Many of patients' behaviours that appear heteronomous are not so. They are assumed, pretended or acquiescent dependencies that form part of patients' strategies for managing practitioners. Some of the behaviours that practitioners call non-compliant are patient's autonomous management of their sickness or condition. Throwing away prescribed medication is one well-known way patients protect their own interests as they see them.[7] Conversely, doctors can feel pressured by patients into prescribing, and 'out of control' of the negotiation.[8] In either case the mutuality of explanation (implied by the idea of collaboration) is missing.

Outside the clinical relationship, institutional customs and policies can constrain both practitioners and patients from finding the kinds and levels of interaction that would suit each's preferred strategies for their management tasks. But institutional constraints are seldom unfortunate circumstances that just happen to be around. (A partial exception to this is in matters of resources.) They tend to favour, or at least not to harm, dominant interests. Institutional customs and norms can be powerful. But they are sustained by people and can be undone by them. Proto-professionals who bring about changes to meet repressed interests show what is possible.

THERAPEUTIC BENEFIT

In the present state of our knowledge, latitude has to be allowed to the term 'therapeutic benefit'. Direct gains in health are often difficult to measure. (Direct losses are usually easier, and consumerists sometimes fall back on them.) Direct gains are still more difficult to tie into causal relationships with single factors, especially the complex ones to do with autonomy. We can identify different kinds of benefit. It can be shown that giving some patients information pre-operatively is significantly correlated with reduction of stress and pain. The patients ask for fewer analgesics after the operation. They seem to get better quicker (Chapter 7). Or it can be shown that people who are given their medical notes or their X-ray pictures lose them less often than hospitals and clinics do (Chapter 8). That makes for speed and safety when someone needs further diagnosis or treatment. That is an indirect therapeutic benefit. Feeling better is a mark of gain in health; so is quicker recovery to a former state of health; more extensive use of damaged parts of the body; a longer time before an irreversible disease recurs; living longer. We can measure some of these things. But we lack a convincing theoretical model of how the factors that might be involved link together to produce the benefit.

In spite of our lack of understanding of those links, we can look at the therapeutic benefits of some standards that support consumers' autonomy in the wide sense, or in the narrow. The next six chapters do that.

Autonomy is too ambiguous a term to use as a category in a discussion of standards of care and treatment. It is more useful to look at some aspects of standards for treatment and care that can be supposed to support autonomy and consumers' varying management styles, and that can be more closely defined. Respect; support; information; control; choice and decision-making itself can each be shown to have therapeutic benefits for some, even most, consumers. Autonomy is like the central figure in a coat of arms, with six supporters holding it up, instead of just two. The six are mutually reinforcing to each other as well as to autonomy. Autonomy is the central figure because it requires and encompasses the others. It is also at the centre because sickness and death confront the autonomous self. They take from, and give meaning to, that self.

5

RESPECT

I do not want to enter the surgery and leave my personhood and capacities outside the door. How can I then use my resources to aid my recovery?

J., a cancer patient (1988)[1]

INTRODUCTION

Staff in the health service are often exhorted to 'treat patients as people' and to recognize 'the person inside the patient'.[2] Sometimes that means with more acknowledgement of their autonomy, sometimes with greater sensitivity to their vulnerability. Either way, patients should not be treated as if they were objects. But what are persons and objects?

A person is the actual self, the unique individual who is experienced subjectively. All other people are objects to the person; they are outside the self, in essence unknowable and uncontrollable. Normally, the sense of autonomous selfhood is sure. But when someone feels ill or is injured or notices a new symptom of disease or disability, part of him or her becomes, as it were, an object to the self. The part is as unknowable and uncontrollable as if it were a non-self, an object. Yet the self knows that this object is connected to it in their shared and inseparable existence. This state of being is almost impossible to describe. Sally Gadow writes about the 'lived body', existing and acting in the world, becoming, when sick, the 'object body';[3] these words get near to some people's experience. Then the self has to manage the object body through the management tasks outlined in Chapter 4. People manage these tasks differently. But to the extent that the self manages the object self, or works for it or on it, it can be called a work-object.

People's work on their work-objects is easily observed. They examine themselves for lumps or changes of colour; they turn the 'clinical gaze' that 'objectifies' onto themselves.[4] They put drops into their eyes to control glaucoma; they measure the levels of sugar in their blood in diabetes; they avoid stressful activities after recovery from mental illness; they assess pain in arthritic joints; and work on themselves in countless other ways. Less easy to see is the more difficult work of managing thought and feeling. Sick people who are too physically dependent to work on themselves much, still have to manage their inner worlds. That can entail managing the boundaries of knowledge, and bringing to bear every resource of emotion and intellect.

■ As soon as the American biologist Stephen Jay Gould recovered from surgery for abdominal mesothelioma, he asked his doctor what to read about this cancer. She said there was nothing worth reading. So Gould called up all the references to mesothelioma in Harvard medical library. The median survival time from discovery was 8 months; that explained the doctor's reluctance to supply references. But Gould decided that his case was probably in the right-hand tail of the curve expressing the variability in survival times, that he would survive much longer than the median time, due to his age, early diagnosis and expert treatment. Ten years later (in 1992) he is still well.[5]

Practitioners, too, see patients both as people and as work-objects.[6]

■ 'I have some patients I must work on.'

GP going to his surgery (1991)[7]

At first, this can seem shocking. Yet everyone is an object to everyone else. And objects can be invested with deep significance and affection. They can be respected. Indeed, it may be easier to respect other objects in the world, sentient and non-sentient, if we do not stipulate that they must be people, before we can treat them with concern and tenderness.

Practitioners and patients can thus be thought of as having four tasks during episodes of sickness or injury or the distressing onset of further disability or disease. They are tasks concerned with the work-object and with the subject-person. They are shown in Table 5.1. They are complex interacting tasks, though some of the work that each does is invisible and unknown to the other.[8]

Between these four tasks there are tensions, ambiguities and uncertainties. There is variation in each practitioner's and each patient's capacity and opportunity to work on their tasks. Patients are often unpractised and unprepared. Or they feel too ill or too

Table 5.1 The four tasks

Practitioners	Patients
practitioners' work *on* patients as work-objects	patients' work *on* themselves as work-objects
practitioners' work *for* and *with* patients as person-subjects*	patients' maintainance *of* themselves as person-subjects

* These are properly person-objects but the term person-subject is probably more congenial to most people.

depressed. Practitioners are practised but sometimes in unfortunate ways. Some practitioners have treated patients as if they were work-objects only, leaving aside recognition of their distress and need for the appearance of concern:[9]

■ A group of doctors subjected a dying baby to repeated echocardiograms, joking and laughing with each other while the baby's father wept.

Other practitioners have treated patients as if they were people only, with little attempt at therapeutic endeavour, at work on the work-object. Much care of people with severe mental handicaps, psychiatric illness or frail old age has been like this. Lack of the technical means to effect cure or rehabilitation or palliation undermines proper work on the work-object. That then tends to affect work for and with the person-subject badly.[10]

On the other hand, a great deal of the care criticized as depersonalized or objectified is simply rude, inconsiderate or cruel. It has nothing to do with tensions round the work-object. Receptionists in out-patient departments who keep talking to each other when someone stands in front of their desk are failing to comply with the norms of ordinary courtesy.

But even when the four tasks are done well, they are difficult. They are hard for practitioners. They remind them of their own vulnerability and mortality. Closeness to another's body and its functions arouses anxiety, disgust, desire and guilt at conscious and unconscious levels, and envy for the care the body is receiving.[11] Closeness to another's thoughts, as when treating people with mental illness or those who show their anxiety or sadness, is frightening and depressing. Doctors and nurses used to be taught 'professional detachment' to enable them to manage their feelings. But detachment has come to be seen as coldness of heart and has been discredited in its old form. No new generally accepted concept-for-practice has taken its place, though 'rational concern' is a possibility.[12]

Working on the work-object is hard for patients, too. It arouses deep anxiety, except for trivial or often repeated work. Sometimes the anxiety is so great that the work can only be done by briefly detaching the work-object from the person-subject. The example of Stephen Jay Gould is exceptional in its clarity. But other people have taken steps of equal difficulty. That we know rather little about most patients' inner workings, and are therefore liable to frustrate rather than facilitate it, is one of the ways the repression of their interests shows.

However these tasks are thought of, and whatever are the feelings that go with them, their boundaries overlap. The patient person-subject is connected to the work-object – is the work-object. Both person-subject and work-object are affected by the practitioner's tasks. The practitioner's tasks are equally inseparable in that the same practitioner carries them out. It is likely that practitioners who seem especially humane combine skill at working on the work-object with capacity for empathetic recognition of the person-subject.[13] They can balance or integrate the two sets of skills and of feelings. (They are the sort of practitioner sought by writer of the quotation that heads this chapter.) They help the patient feel that recovery is possible. Recovery may be of health. Or it may be of a sense of the person-self as transcending the work-object.

The rest of this chapter gives examples of standards of treatment and care that enhance or diminish practitioners' and patients' work on their tasks. Some of the examples could be put in another category; they overlap because of the connections between the tasks. Lack of care in any of them is liable to be seen by consumers and consumerists as lack of respect. Patients' interests may be oppressed or suppressed if that care is not taken. If it is taken, it is welcomed and remembered.

■ 'We must . . . learn to promote mental and emotional wellbeing in the face of physical illness, whether it be acute, chronic and disabling, or life threatening. Simple interventions based on the patient's wishes may have more far-reaching therapeutic effects than biomedicine can measure.'
Doctor, after acute serious illness, during which her wish to keep her baby beside her in hospital had been met (1990)[14]

(Practitioners' respect for person-subject)

■ 'In hospital I am in "a safe place" . . . and am able to relax . . . I keep my own medication by my bedside and have to patiently work out my dosages.'

> Nurse with Parkinson's disease, recovering from an episode of destablization (1989)[15]

(Practitioners' respect for patients' work on work-object)

RESPECT FOR THE WORK-OBJECT

The maintenance of physical and physiological integrity

Some patterns of care weaken, harm or distress the work-object. We have moved away from some of the extreme harshness of earlier centuries – the bleedings, purgings, hot and cold treatments, drug-induced comas. But there are new uncomfortable or risky treatments and diagnostic tests, justified by today's belief in their efficacy. There are also blind spots of insensitivity in everyday care, supported by medical or nursing beliefs that contradict common sense and biomedical knowledge.

Both consumerists and professionals criticize harsh routines. As well as considering that routine interventions in labour are clinically harmful and liable to lead to a 'cascade of intervention', consumerists in maternity care have perceived hidden meanings in those routine practices. Thus shaving the pubic area can be seen as signifying a woman's reversion to a prepubertal state, and denial of her adult status; enemas as invasion of private body space; and induction or acceleration of labour as taking control over a process that belongs to the woman and her baby. Lack of respect for the work-object blends into lack of respect for the person-subject. That is partly why consumerists, guided by their ideologies, pick out these sorts of practices. They offend against consumers' autonomy, as well as against their clinical welfare and their health.

There are some routines in surgical care that are like those in maternity care. Criticism of them has remained largely with professionals, for in spite of the vastly greater number of operations performed every year than babies born, consumerists have given scant attention to general surgery performed on both men and women. They will probably be slow to do so until the speciality attracts attention from some ideological or interest group comparable to the feminism that has influenced maternity and women's health consumer pressure groups.

Shaving the site of an operation was shown in USA in 1971 to increase infection rates, not decrease them.[16] Again, shaving a strip of scalp will generally suffice for surgery on the head; but shaving the whole head continues in some hospitals.[17] The detriments are discomfort from new hair growing in, loss of body heat, and the embarrassment, even shame, of a shaven head.

Fasting is another routine that can harm the work-object. Preventing patients from eating or drinking before a general anaesthetic is a precaution against their choking on vomit. Fasting only needs to last for as long as normal physiological processes take to empty the stomach, 6 hours at most. But patients due for operation are often fasted from midnight the day before, whatever the times their operations are scheduled. So in some hospitals all patients are fasted for at least 8 hours, and some much longer. This is debilitating even for healthy young adults. Elderly patients may become dangerously dehydrated before the operation. This can be corrected by an intravenous infusion set up to compensate for loss of body fluids during the operation; but only if the amount lost is known, which it usually is not. Some nurses have suggested that this physiological derangement could account for the confusion and disturbed bodily functioning seen in some elderly people after surgery.[18] About 20 years have passed since the first observations on this subject were made. But protracted pre-operative fasting persists.

Institutional routines and practices, as well as clinical ones, disrupt normal sleep patterns and circadian rhythms. The early awakening of patients in many hospitals is notorious. But it continues; and patients continue to complain about it. Circadian rhythms are affected by days' length. So nursing patients in rooms without windows or under lights that are left on all the time can be detrimental to them.[19] Some labour rooms, intensive care units, and special care nurseries for babies have been built in disregard of this knowledge.

Another issue that concerns consumerists is the routine use of high doses of psychotropic drugs. Many psychotropic drugs take days or weeks to become fully effective. That makes it difficult to change their dosage quickly. But heavy medication can leave patients 'too clouded in the head to feel able to talk or deal with feelings subsequently'.[20] That is, they cannot work on the work-object.

RESPECT FOR THE PERSON-SUBJECT

Status

How people are addressed reflects the status accorded them. Modes of addressing or referring to patients; how they are labelled on their wrists, doors or beds; casual greetings in corridors, are all contentious issues in health care. Many consumerists deplore any hint of downgrading patients' status from adult to child or to social inferior. They see the use of patients' names without titles; the use of their first names alone; promiscuous endearments; baby talk ('pop up on the bed'); and patronizing or incomprehensible synonyms ('water works', 'tail') as at best demeaning. At worst, they see them as a sinister parade of power and pretence. But many staff see the same usages as expressing friendliness and equality between themselves and patients. They are unaware that some patients feel mortified or angry, or dislike relationships that they perceive as lacking in respect and sincerity. Such deep divisions over intentions and interpretations mean that neither side can prevail easily. The highest standard, consumerists and many professionals agree, is that patients should be asked how they prefer to be addressed. Compliance with that standard is variable:[21]

■ When a nurse addressed an elderly lady the day before her death as Winnie, rather than by her title and surname, or even her proper first name, Winifred, she protested. This is an example of a patient's work to maintain the person-subject in the face of the threat of staff's failure to respect it.

The surroundings in which care is given also reflect the respect accorded to patients. Many long-stay institutions have a barren ugliness. Some GPs' surgeries are cramped. Even in moderately genial surroundings dictatorial notices abound ('Do not knock on the door'; 'Report to the receptionist on your arrival'). Everywhere are the outward and visible signs of an inward lack of respect for patients' status as competent and valued adults.

Control of the boundaries round the self

In everyday life people control the physical and psychological boundaries round themselves by dividing their time between private and public places; by distinguishing between public and private acts; by using words and signs to indicate what physical and emotional proximity or distance is desired; by controlling how much new information reaches them, censoring unpleasant or upsetting images, searching for words, sounds or images that comfort or inspire; and by controlling what they tell and show other people about themselves. This management of the boundaries between the self and the objects in the outer world, in their richness and their threat, is crucial to the self's well-being.

When people become patients they have less control over the boundaries round the self. Work-objects cannot be private; practitioners' access to them is necessary. But there are ways in which patients' loss of control over boundaries, and the effects of this loss, can be kept to a minimum. Nurses in hospital and the community often manage those ways well.

Symbolic private space

Giving patients privacy is the most obvious way of helping them maintain their control. Privacy for consultations; private rooms; 'personal space' for patients in multi-bedded wards, when staff must ask permission to enter the space, as if it were a private room; there are many familiar examples. Less obvious are some others.

Controlling impingements from other people

Sensitively grouping patients at various stages of recovery; letting patients choose their companions in day rooms and dining rooms; offering group activities but not compelling them; giving patients contacts for self-help groups in the community, help patients control their own boundaries.

Controlling information

Helping patients control what kind of information reaches them is more difficult. What patients cannot control, staff have to take responsibility for managing. Threatening objects raise conscious apprehension and stimulate unconscious anxieties. Macabre jokes, like a vampire drawn on the door of a room where patients have blood samples drawn off, must be foregone. But there are dilemmas with equipment that can be interpreted as either alarming or reassuring. Does a baby resuscitator in a labour room suggest problems or safety? Every aspect of the surroundings needs to be scrutinized for its messages. But although it is unwise to suggest that bad things can happen, it is wrong to conceal them when they have. Drawing the curtains round all the beds in a ward where someone has died makes patients uneasy. Reality is better than fantasy.

A predictable and facilitating environment

Institutional and clinical routines help staff feel secure and in control of events, knowing what is going to happen. That is why some routines are retained in spite of harm to patients. Regularity and predictability is important to patients for the same reason.[22] Meals should be on time; doctors' regular visits prompt; a test at 10.30 a.m., not 'sometime tomorrow'. Predictability helps patients work on themselves as work-objects, by preventing suspense and unnecessary anxiety. Delayed or erratic visits from doctors are especially harmful in situations where avoidable anxiety is strongly iatrogenic, like in-patient antenatal care and psychiatric care.

That clocks and calendars should be visible in psychiatric wards was one of the early standards enunciated by the pressure group MIND.[23] Since poor 'orientation in time' is taken as a sign of mental illness or impairment, it is paradoxical that stopped clocks and out-of-date calendars figure in some wards. Institutions have an obligation to stick to reality. Confusion locks, intended to foil elderly patients' attempts to leave the ward by contradicting their expectation that specific actions have specific results, are another example. To destroy the predictability and responsiveness of the inanimate world, and to separate consequences from actions, is to undermine patients' work on themselves as persons and as work-objects.

SHARING THE WORK-OBJECT

Detachment and attachment

Some patients, in some situations, find professional detachment and an impersonal manner helpful. They find it supports their dignity, threatened by the vicissitudes of bodily functioning.[24] Other patients value closeness between themselves and prac-titioners, sharing the work-object during intimate caring.[25] So it looks as if consumers need some means of assessing professionals' personal styles and feelings, to make a choice where that is possible.

Sharing information about the work object

In the early nineteenth century, new instruments like the stethoscope enabled doctors to make observations of patients' physiological state, independently of what patients could observe and report for themselves. X-rays at the end of the nineteenth century began to do the same for patients' anatomy. The doctor's knowledge of the body as a work-object became different from the patient's. And it could be withheld from him or her. That gave doctors new power over patients. By closing off knowledge about the work-object, it also undermined patients as person-subjects, able to work on the work-object. All new diagnostic technologies have potential for increasing this alienation of the person-subject from the work-object. (So they are often called depersonalizing.) But many new technologies also have the potential for increasing patients' ability to work on the work-object. (So they could equally be called de-objectifying – diminishing the opacity of the work-object.) 'Good' practitioners (good by consumers' and proto-professional standards) offer to show patients their X-rays, ultrasound scans, temperature charts and so on, and share their interpretations with them.

SHARING THE PERSON-SUBJECT

There is some evidence that reminding staff that patients are people, autonomous people who have been used to health and activity, can help them give better care:[26]

■ Photographs of patients, looking as they did before illness, caused nurses in an intensive care unit to perceive them more favourably: 19 out of 20 nurses replying to a questionnaire agreed that 'the personality and character of the patient are emphasized by photographs'; 18 that seeing a picture of the patient in normal health gave a goal to aim for; and 19 that the photo helped the nurse 'to relate to the patient as an individual'; 13 thought that the comparison between the photograph and the patient could be upsetting. (That illustrates the tension caused by juxtaposing the idea of a person-subject against the helpless, perhaps unconscious, work-object, in an experiment like this.) Though only three nurses thought that better nursing care was given as a result of seeing the photographs, the author was convinced that it had.

'Stripping' patients of the signs of the value that they, and more especially other people, put on them – their clothes, their jewellry, their small possessions – has long been acknowledged as detrimental to their sense of themselves as people.[27] Yet it continues.

■ Lockable bedside lockers are uncommon in most hospitals, so precious and private things are difficult to keep safe. Cards are strung on lines above the bedfoot, out of reach of elderly patients. Flowers are sometimes removed from bedsides to the middle of the ward. Or they are rearranged by flower ladies to their own taste. Sometimes flowers are pronounced dead and thrown away, before they are; a curious symbolism.

Things like these reflect the shortcomings of some health care; its lack of respect for the ordinary and the human.

6

SUPPORT

There are no 'visiting hours' – you can come at any time of the day or night and we are glad to see you.

Leaflet for children's ward, Charing Cross Hospital,
London (no date, 1970s)

Respect for consumers entails respecting their accustomed sources of support; honouring the support they receive from the people to whom they are connected in friendship or love. In gathering sick people together, away from their everyday life, hospitals in western countries broke those connections between people. Relatives and friends were redefined as 'visitors', with the psychological and spatial distance and the temporariness that implies. Although in hospitals' early days visitors were taken for granted, by the mid-nineteenth century they were excluded or allowed in for brief 'visiting hours' only.[1] The germ theory of infectious disease; staff's growing power in professional and semi-professional groups; their shaping of their workplace, the hospital, to suit their needs and wishes; and their growing confidence in the effectiveness of their treatments and in themselves as 'caring' people led to a belief that visitors were dangerous to patients and a nuisance to staff. Separation from relatives and friends became part of treatment and care.

Some of the earliest work of consumer pressure groups was directed towards securing patients' access to the people to whom they turn for support. (I shall call these people 'relations'; they may be parents, spouses, relatives or close friends – people with whom a relationship of reciprocity, continuity and shared experiences exists or, for babies, is beginning.) Consumerists and proto-professionals articulate and press for standards that:

● extend daily 'visiting hours' for all patients in hospital;

- include accommodation at night, and moderate comfort during the day, for the relations of babies, children, the very ill and the dying;
- ensure the presence of relations at times of special stress, like consultation and diagnosis; childbirth; pre- and post-operative periods; the induction of and recovery from anaesthesia; treatments, including those in out-patient and accident and emergency departments; and in the hour of death;
- in maternity care, keep babies by their mothers' beds, and under their charge, rather than removed against the mothers' wishes to a nursery; in paediatric and geriatric care, provide a bed next to the patient's for parent or spouse;
- remove restrictions on parents' access to their babies in special and intensive care baby units; on children visiting their parents or grandparents in acute or geriatric wards; on brothers and sisters of the new or prospective baby visiting maternity units; and on children, uncles and aunts and grandparents going into special or intensive care baby units.

Although all patients' free access to relations has not yet been achieved, the trend to restore each to the other is set. This access is important for reasons that follow from the discussion of respect; reasons to do with the person-subject and the work-object. The reasons change in emphasis with patients' ages and situations. But some general points can be made.

The presence of a relation protects the self from loneliness and isolation, from the fear of abandonment or desertion. This can be seen most clearly in the very young, where this fear is called 'separation anxiety'. But even adults, and perhaps especially older adults, can be afraid that they will lose their value and significance to other people. At the same time, the relations' presence strengthens the self through the esteem, concern and love that his or her presence implies. For the very young child, the relation partly 'contains' and manages some of the child's feelings of distress. For an older child or for an adult, touch and other non-verbal communication retain their power to comfort. But talk, of course, becomes crucial. Some patients manage their thoughts and feelings through repeated rehearsals and reinterpretations of their experiences:[2]

■ A young woman having treatment for breast cancer telephoned her husband as soon as he returned home, though they had been talking to each other up till the end of visiting hours.

At another level, the presence of a relation buffers the self from harsh or intrusive aspects of the environment. This is especially important for children. The relation can soften frightening or disagreeable events by explaining things in ways the child can understand; by showing confidence in the staff carrying out the procedures; or by suggesting minor changes or delays until the child is ready. But adults do this for other adults, too. So a wife may ask for pain relief for her husband or try to find out what the treatment plan is. If care seems too bad, a determined relation can remove the patient from it:[3]

■ 'When I saw the way the nurse held him to feed him, I went through the roof! We brought him home.'

Mother of baby with spina bifida

That quotation points to staff's behaviour as a possible source of distress to patients. The presence of relatives or friends inevitably affects staff. Inconsiderate behaviour towards the patients is less likely (though irritability or unkindness towards visitors may take its place). More positively, relatives' or friends' presence affirms the patient's social worth and status. This is especially important for elderly, disabled or mentally ill people; for people who are liable to be stigmatized or towards whom staff may have unconscious feelings of fear or dislike. So at this level, the presence of relations helps patients in the task of managing practitioners' work upon them.

The other side of visiting, its effects on practitioners' work and feelings, is equally complex. Relations are a threat to practitioners' ways of doing things, to their control over their work-objects and to their definitions of the situation. So practitioners fear that relatives and friends will interfere in patients' treatment: give sweets to children before an operation; smuggle in drugs to adolescents; trip over apparatus; make upsetting remarks; listen to confidential conversations. This fear corresponds to relations' suspicion that staff will treat patients carelessly or roughly. Both sides attribute bad motives and actions to each other, as rare instances of unfortunate conduct are converted in conversation into common events.

Visitors may also seem to undermine the rewards practitioners gain from their work. Practitioners, especially nurses, sometimes believe that they can substitute for patients' relations. Nurses can take on the specialized caring and therapeutic roles movingly

Table 6.1 Stages in the acceptance of standards for children's access to their relations, 1951–1991

Year	Government guidance	Survey	Visiting arrangements found	
1951		Ministry of Health	½ hour daily: no visiting: other:	43% 23% 34%
1959	*HM(59)19.* Platt Report accepted: parents in ward at any reasonable time, mothers should be admitted with child under 5 years			
1962		NAWCH	½–5 hours, afternoons only, very little accommodation for parents	
1966	*HM(66)18.* Fixed visiting should be abandoned; hospitals should help mothers stay in			
1969		NAWCH	'unrestricted' in daytime: no visiting in a.m.: other:	5% 25% 8%
1971	*HM(71)22.* Visiting without restriction is essential			
1973		NAWCH	24 hour access: 10–15 hours: 7–9 hours: 4–6 hours: 0–3 hours:	19% 32% 33% 14% 2%
1976	*HC(76)18.* The need for unrestricted visiting in children's wards and the desirability of providing overnight accommodation for parents was described in HM(71)22			
1983		NAWCH	24 hour access: other:	49% 51%
1986		NAWCH re-survey of worst wards in 1983 survey	24 hour access: 'visiting hours': restriction on day of operation:	85% 11% 4%
1991	Department of Health. Parents are not visitors, they should be encouraged to be with their child at all times			

described by Patricia Benner and Judith Wrubel in *The Primacy of Caring*.[4] There nurses interpret illness and treatment to patients and help support them through it, drawing on clinical expertise as well as on good feeling. Staff's presence, skill and care is necessary at times of stress or risk, for clinical purposes and for reassurance. But what they give is complementary to the patients' accustomed relationships. Staff cannot substitute for relations, cannot take their place. Many have never thought they could. But in neonatal, paediatric and geriatric care, nurses have sometimes believed that their relationships with patients were more significant than is possible. Between possessiveness and detachment is an area that some staff have found difficult to manage. Patients' constant access to their relations can make this painfully evident to practitioners. It can force them to see that some of the good they wish to do, cannot be done by them.

Visiting is therefore a focus of deep conflicts of feelings and of interests. It is hardly surprising that consumer groups who suggest that visiting hours be extended, or individual relatives or friends who ask to visit outside official visiting times, are sometimes refused.

It is the task of consumer pressure groups, working for suppressed or oppressed interests, to combat that refusal. When consumerists or proto-professionals set about trying to raise the standards for access to relations for a specific care group, the processes they start are in some ways simple. Only certain actions are relevant to their campaigns. But the issues open up complex stages in the development of sensibility, argument, research and the re-definition of interests. The stages are outlined here, though they can occur in various overlapping and repetitive orders. The progress of the acceptance of NAWCH's standards for children's access to relations is used as illustration. Those stages span more than 30 years, and are still incomplete. Table 6.1 summarizes their course. Some standards for access have been developed and accepted more quickly. Others are going more slowly.

1 Restrictions on 'visiting' are in place or are introduced. Everything starts from restriction. As restrictions are lifted for some categories of patients, new specialized care attracts new restrictions. Thus parents were excluded at first from nurseries for healthy newborn babies, then allowed in. This was repeated when special care baby units for premature or sick infants were

introduced. Similarly, visiting is now more restricted in many intensive care and coronary care units than in general medical wards.

2 Patients' distress begins to be observed. Practitioners are often insensitive to distress, or rather, they can quickly learn to distance themselves from it and disregard it.[5] Filming the distress and providing words to describe it can break through professional defences. James Robertson's films of young children in hospital, in the 1950s, were models of that approach.[6]

3 'Public concern' may build up. Public concern may only mean an article or letter in a newspaper; but it may be enough to mobilize dissatisfaction, expressed through a consumer group or a professional or government working party.

4 A set of theoretical arguments for change is articulated. It is difficult to frame a case about something that touches people so deeply. What Ian Suttie more than 50 years ago called the 'taboo on tenderness' still exists.[7] It is a defensive denial of feeling throughout society, not just in some professionals. One of its consequences is that the mere statement of feeling, however eloquent, often has little effect. It has to be supported by argument; and that argument may seem exaggerated or irrelevant to those who do not acknowledge the feeling.

5 Evidence from other disciplines is called on to support the theoretical arguments. Bowlby's work on young children deprived of their mothers' care during the Second World War, and Harlow's work on infant monkeys removed from their mothers, showed detriments to normal development. Both were influential in paediatric and maternity pressure groups.[8,9] The work on monkeys, especially, was much quoted by members in their presentations to lay and professional groups. It was perhaps easier for them and their audiences to empathize with the blameless monkeys than with the morally more complex humans.

6 Surveys of current policies and practices are made. If surveys shows widespread restrictions, publishing that can stimulate concern and action.

7 Consumer pressure groups and proto-professionals try to persuade the Department of Health to articulate a standard, or a new higher standard, for the practice. The Department may then issue guidance to health authorities about standards.

8 Practitioners and clinical research workers play a key part. They

undertake clinical research relevant to the consumerists' desired standard:[10]

■ An ENT surgeon, D. J. Brain and a psychiatrist, Inga Maclay, conducted the first clinical trial of the effects of mothers' presence in hospital on their children's recovery from surgery. 101 and 96 children admitted to Rubery Hill Hospital, Birmingham for tonsill-ectomy and (or) adenoidectomy in 1967 were allocated at random to an experimental group, mothers staying in hospital, or a control group, limited visiting by mothers. The experimental group made a more satisfactory adjustment to hospital and were less disturbed after their return home (both statistically significant differences for the measures used). Most importantly, and from strictly clinical data, 23 per cent of the control children had a post-operative haemorrhage or infection, significantly more than the 11 per cent of the experimental group.

The lower infection rate in children whose mothers lived in and looked after them was probably partly due to a reduction in cross infection from staff. Current thinking would also attribute some part of it to protection from stress. Infection is almost always the first argument against giving patients access to relations. But research shows that infection rates are either lower when access is given or no higher.[11]

NAWCH sent the report of this work, published in the *British Medical Journal* in 1968, to its local groups across the country. Also included was *The Story of Dawn*, a harrowing account of a child who cried inconsolably and died from a post-operative haemorrhage after a tonsillectomy, while her mother was nearby but forbidden to go to her.[12]

This research made the case for unrestricted access, though there had been earlier observations that pointed in the same direction. As with other clinical trials, replication may be unethical if the first one has shown distinct benefits or detri-ments.

9 Acceptance of the standard spreads.
10 Other studies show further benefits to patients:[13]

■ In 1989 two paediatricians, M.R.H. Taylor and P. O'Connor in Dublin, found that the stay in hospital of children with living-in parents was 31 per cent shorter than that of children whose parents spent the day in hospital, but not the night. Of 586 admissions for any of 12 medical conditions, 136 children with resident parents had a mean stay of 2.88 days whereas children without resident parents had a mean stay of 4.16 days. As length of stay is a proxy indicator for health status, it can be assumed that the former group got better more quickly than the latter. Accommodation was offered to all parents, and more readily accepted by those in higher socio-economic groups, but the findings held good within each socio-economic group.

11 Consumerists may try to safeguard the new standard by getting it defined as a legal right or included in patients' charters.
12 The new standard may be written into specifications for agreements for services between provider and purchaser health authorities. These specifications, introduced into the NHS in 1991, mean that detailed standards can be included in both provider and purchaser documents. The *NAWCH Quality Review, Setting Standards for Children in Health Care* (1989) was cited in some specifications for 1991 and 1992. It includes the standard, set out as one of ten basic rights in a charter, that:[14]

> Children in hospital shall have the right to have their parents with them at all times provided this is in the best interest of the child. Accommodation should therefore be offered to all parents, and they should be helped and encouraged to stay. In order to share in the care of their child, parents should be fully informed about ward routine and their active participation encouraged.

This standard was re-affirmed in new Department of Health Guidance in 1991:[15]

> Districts and provider hospitals are advised to agree service specifications which recognise that parents and members of the immediate family are not visitors and encourage and assist them to be with their child at all times unless the interests of the child preclude this. . . .

13 The new standard is incorporated into patterns of care. The benefits once hesitantly attributed to it are stated as self-evident, needing no justification or evidence in their support. (The old standards become curiosities, half forgotten.)
14 That remains so until new issues are identified and new interests defined. Then the processes begin again until the standard is superseded by new patterns of care or new standards.

The NAWCH standards have gained acceptance, as far as they have, because of the intense effort put into that acceptance by

NAWCH members, locally and nationally, by other consumerists and by proto-professionals. Undoubtedly, there are issues of access to relations in other care groups that have not been identified yet or have attracted too little political or therapeutic attention to be moved forward. Access to relations for adult patients is an example on the borderline between suppressed and oppressed interests. The Patients Association did some work early in the 1960s, pressing successfully for the extension of visiting hours for adult and geriatric patients. But it has not taken the work further. Community Health Councils' national body, ACHCEW, has enunciated the standard.[16]

> All persons have a right to . . . the support of a relative or friend at any time.
>
> *Patients' Charter* (1986).

But CHCs have often been satisfied with restricted visiting. The promise that staff will be flexible about visiting hours sometimes reassures them; but even one instance of capricious refusal vitiates the promise:[17]

> Let us have free visiting for people. Is there a NAWCH for the over 16s?
>
> Letter to *Nursing Times* from nurse whose husband was a patient (1979)

It is sad that 'ordinary' intuitive knowledge about support is disregarded until it can be validated by research.[18] But research can show some valuable things. Thus there is evidence that loving support has even more striking therapeutic effects than might have been supposed. The work comes from observations on babies, not children or adults, and from an extreme and tragic situation. But it is often from extreme situations that most can be learnt:[19]

■ The brief lives of babies born with inoperable spina bifida at a hospital in North Staffordshire between 1971 and 1981 were reviewed. Until 1976 it had been doctors' and nurses' policy to prevent parents from taking their babies home. Staff had discouraged parents from caring for the babies in the hospital, or even from visiting them, and had advised against becoming fond of them. But in 1976 one couple insisted on taking their baby home. Gradually other parents did the same and staff began to give parents the choice of having their baby home or leaving him or her in hospital. A research worker interviewed the parents of 44 babies, 26 who had stayed in hospital and 18 who had been taken home. The babies had lived between 8 days and 8 months.

The parents who had taken their babies home judged them to have had a better quality of life, felt less regret and bitterness, and suffered less in the long term than the parents who had not been allowed to take the babies home. But above all, the babies who had been looked after at home lived signficantly longer than those who had stayed in hospital. That there were many uncontrolled variables is certain. But one mother's words are equally certain:[20]

Love kept her alive.

7

INFORMATION

. . . only the patient is aware of how much information he wants to know if life is to go on at a productive level.

Cancer patient (1988)[1]

INTRODUCTION

Information is an evident political good. It has the power to help consumers protect their interests if those are threatened by oppression or suppression. It is to many people an ethical good, part of their life's search for truth. It can be a therapeutic good, guiding consumers in their tasks of managing themselves and the professionals round them. But information inaccurately or thoughtlessly given is a political, ethical and therapeutic detriment. So information is contentious.

Consumerists will always believe that consumers want more information than they are willingly given by professionals. Professionals will believe that consumers want less than consumerists suppose. There is abundant evidence that consumers want more than they commonly get.[2] How much more remains obscure, for the act of offering information prevents a return to the state of unknowing that an individual consumer might have preferred. Information, unlike choice, cannot be rescinded or forgotten.

As well as difficulties in deciding what consumers 'really' want to know, there are others. There are problems of vocabulary and the 'knowledge gap'. Consumerists think those problems are exaggerated. They find little difficulty in explaining things to consumers.[3] And there is evidence that professionals believe that consumers' ignorance and inability to remember what is said to them are greater than they are.[4] There is the doctrine of 'therapeutic privilege', the belief that withholding information can be justified if giving it might lead a patient to reject treatment or to feel alarm.[5] Many people, consumers and professionals, call that paternalism, and reject it.[6] Then there practical problems: practitioners' lack of time to answer the questions that even straightforward information engenders (about the minor side effects of treatment, for example); sometimes practitioners' own ignorance or misunderstanding; practitioners' and patients' ambivalence over telling and hearing bad news; and an overall lack of practice and skill in managing such conversations.

It thus comes about that consumerists' and professionals' standards for giving information are likely to conflict. Consumerists want consumers to be offered 'full information'. That means information given as accurately, in as much detail, and at the time, that consumers ask for, or expect, it. (That standard implies a second; that clinical consultations and conversations should take place within a context or atmosphere of responsiveness that makes it easy for consumers to ask.) So it leaves the control of information ultimately with the consumer. Thus the ACHCEW standard in their patients' charter is that patients should be given[7]

> Full information on all aspects of their condition and proposed care (including the alternatives available), unless they express a wish to the contrary.

Many professionals prefer 'structured information': information given at their discretion. In some provider health authorities, that phrase in ACHCEW's standard has been altered to read[8]

> at the discretion of the responsible consultant.

This conflict is difficult to resolve. Many consumerists see it chiefly in terms of power. Many professionals see it as conflict between the ethical good of lucidity (patients' rights to know all the relevant details about the situation they find themselves in) and of beneficence (professionals' duty to do patients no harm). Resolving the conflict at the level of patient and practitioner probably requires an explicit lead by the practitioner. He or she could say that a life-threatening or disabling disease is a possibility (if it is), and give an assurance that the patient will be told the truth if he or she asks, but is free not to ask.[9] Leaving it to the patient to ask questions when he or she does not know what kinds of diseases are possible, nor perhaps what words to use, puts him or her at too great a disadvantage. Fumbling questions can get ambiguous, euphemistic or evasive replies that may satisfy practitioners' ethical obligation to answer questions put to them, but that seriously mislead and frustrate patients.[10] But announcing a serious disease without leaving the patient the choice of not knowing about it can be distressing in a different way.

These kinds of conflicts are played out round four kinds of information: information about patients themselves and their diagnoses; about the disease or condition and its prognosis; about what will be experienced during investigation, treatment or care; and about possible courses of treatment or care. The last will be discussed in Chapter 9, on choice, the others here.

KINDS OF INFORMATION

Information about the self and about diagnosis

Information about a patient's condition and diagnosis are closely connected. It is worth wondering how clinical practice, and our views of health and sickness, would have developed if practitioners had never closed off knowledge of the work-object from patients (Chapter 5) but had continued to rely on simple observations and on what patients could tell them.[11] Would early consumers have insisted on contributing different definitions of reality to the discourse or would they have fallen under its power more completely than have today's consumers?

Given that technological aids to diagnosis can be useful, consumerist and proto-professional standards encourage the prompt, and where feasible, the instantaneous, sharing of diagnostic data and their interpretation.

■ Antenatal ultrasound can be used in threatened miscarriage to ascertain whether the foetus is alive or dead. If the latter, the woman can see this straight away (from its lack of response to stimuli) and begin to come to terms with bereavement. If there is no foetus (a blighted ovum), the woman can see that the foetus did not die, but rather never existed.[12] That is a different sort of bereavement, for some women less sad.

■ Using a video-colposcope for examination of the cervix allows a woman (and her partner if she wishes) to see what the doctor sees. Some women are as adept as the doctor at picking up abnormal patches on the cervix.[13]

Unfortunately, there is a grey area in diagnostics when procedures are carried out by practitioners or by technicians who may not be authorized to show or interpret images or data to patients, or even to answer questions about why the procedure is being done. Formulating new standards that respect patients' wishes and their ownership of the work-object is urgent.

■ 287 patients who had a barium meal or barium enema answered a questionnaire asking whether they would wish to know the result immediately. 269 said yes; 5 no; 13 did not know.[14]

In nursing, changes towards sharing information with patients are taking place too, though not as quickly as all patients would like:[15]

> When I asked for information about my health, I was met with, at best, surprise and, at worst resentment . . . [Nurses] seemed to think that knowledge of my condition was a privilege that I, as a mere layman, could not be trusted with.
>
> Man, brief stay in hospital for diagnosis (1990)

Examples of better progress are:

■ In some acute and geriatric wards, and especially in Nursing Development Units, patients can choose to keep the nursing notes at their bedside; or have access to them when they ask; or not to see them.[16]

■ In a dermatology ward in the Queen's Medical Centre, Nottingham, patients write their own care plans (e.g. how many times a day dressings will be changed, when they will apply ointment) or dictate them to a nurse. This requires preliminary explanation and discussion between nurse and patient. This in turn helps patients understand and follow their treatment. Drawings of the structure of skin; diagrams of the legs' vascular system (for venous ulcers); charts about the potency of the different drugs used on skin and how to apply them; coloured photographs of various skin cancers, and information about other dermatological topics are prominent.[17] The skin is one of the body's most visible and accessible organs (as well as the largest) so it lends itself well to this open approach. But the idea of increasing patients' ability to locate and visualize other organs and parts of the body, and their lesions or dysfunctions, could well be extended to those who would like that insight.

Health-care professionals call these innovations 'patient education' and self-care. They are those. But I prefer to think of them as the restoration of the work-object to the person-subject. Put another way, these new standards treat patients as people.

Information about the disease, injury or condition

Giving patients the correct technical name of their disease or condition is an important consumerist and proto-professional standard.

Only with that name can consumers begin to draw on the sources of information around them. The story of Stephen Jay Gould in Chapter 5 is an example of someone bringing exceptional resources of scientific knowledge and logical thought to bear on the work-object. It goes almost without saying that the outcome cannot always be as happy. But the appeal of alternative and complementary medicine for some patients lies partly in their encouragement of an instrumental approach to the work-object. A special diet or exercises becomes an active discipline, a doing something, as well as a vehicle for the open discussion of the disease, its prognosis and treatment.

In mental illness, a diagnostic name is important for another reason. Patients need to know how they are perceived by staff in order to work on their own behaviour, to the extent that they can. Patients also need to know the diagnostic name, and what staff take it to signify, in order to challenge the diagnosis (if they wish). Some mental illness patients are considered by staff to 'lack insight' into their condition because they have never been told what staff consider it to be.

Written information for consumers about their disease or condition is increasingly published by self-help and by professional groups. Doctors in Nottingham who produced a booklet *Living with Achalasia* (an incurable, benign disease of the oesophagus) concluded after surveying patients who had read it, that patients 'do not want to be shielded from unpleasant aspects of the disease'.[18] They particularly wanted to know about the long-term prognosis and the slightly increased risk of developing cancer. As rated by themselves, patients' anxiety decreased in over one-third of the 126 respondents, but increased in 6 per cent.

Self-help and consumer groups' publications occasionally include warnings about doctors – 'Not all are sympathetic or easy to talk to' – as well as information that is intended to make up for their presumed deficits.[19] Consumerists think it desirable for consumers to have a range of publications, so that they can find information, or an approach, that suits them. Some professionals feel they can only offer publications whose contents they approve.

Investigation, treatment and care

Major decisions about diagnostic tests or about treatment are made, except in emergencies, before patients come into hospital.

Discussions of types of procedure, whether X-rays may be taken, whether a blood transfusion might or will be given, should take place then. They are requirements for informed consent, and increasingly seen as such. Discussion also enables patients to make any reservations or requests that they consider in their interests, e.g. for an autologous blood transfusion (storing and using the patient's blood instead of someone else's – it carries less risk of infection or of damage to the immune system).

Where there is a series of procedures, treatments or tests, scheduled over time, consumerists hold that the full schedule should be unveiled from the first. Fertility investigations;[20] treatment after examination by colposcopy; tests of metabolic function; courses of radiotherapy; sequential operations to correct skeleto-muscular or cardiac defects are examples. It is usually thought to be better to omit steps that turn out to be needless than to introduce unheralded ones. Pre-admission visits, common in hospital maternity care, even videos of what to expect, have their place, too.

These sorts of foreknowledge enable consumers to use their resources of time and knowledge to adjust themselves and some-times the procedures to their view of their own interests. Professionals may think that their loss of control outweighs any possible gain to consumers. The following comments make this conflict clear:[21]

■ Over and above the necessity for admitting patients [to hospital], there are advantages that come from the same sources as the harmful effects [to self-esteem]. Most patients adapt to being admitted . . . and may come to terms with their disease and its implications for the first time. After 'institutionalisation' has occurred they are prepared to accept advice which they would not have taken as outpatients.

Once treatment has been agreed between practitioner and patient, there is evidence of distinct therapeutic benefits from information. The best evidence comes from research into pre-operative care and post-operative recovery. When patients are told what will happen to them, what they will see, and what sensations they will experience, many show less anxiety, have fewer post-operative complications, need less pain relief and make a quicker recovery than those who have not been so briefed.[22,23]

Such ordinary information, sometimes grandly called 'psycho-educational intervention', can be supposed to help patients feel less uncertainty; have fewer unrealistic anxieties and trepidations; do some of the 'work of worrying' about real risks and dangers in advance;[24] make better sense of what is happening; and feel a greater sense of control. This sense of control is called 'cognitive control' and can be developed by encouraging patients to dwell on the positive rather than the negative aspects of the surgery they are to undergo. That too can have beneficial effects on their recovery.[25]

During these explanations from staff, patients can ask questions and get to know the anaesthetist and other theatre staff. So they are more likely to feel treated 'as people' with rational concerns and preferences. That is support to the person-subject.

As would be expected where biopsychosocial factors come in, some patients benefit more than others from information given pre-operatively, as measured by self-report and by psychological and physiological tests. Research to find out which patients will benefit and which will not, is confused by different operational definitions and by uncontrolled variables in the environment. But patients who are 'monitors' want to find out and discuss what will happen. Those who are 'blunters' want to avoid information.[26] These coping strategies are an aspect of each person's preferred management style. Most people can probably adjust the amount of information they want very finely. So many patients could probably identify their own preferred styles, if invited to do so. Since practitioners regard assessing patients' needs for information as part of their professional task, there should be an opportunity for sharing the identification of a patient's preferred style.

Some American surgeons give patients videos of their operations. (Home videos of childbirth are a precedent. But whether fathers should make videos during hospital deliveries is controversial in the UK.) Seeing the operation can be supposed to help them integrate their experiences into their lives. Information can serve the past and heal it, as well as preparing the future.

Conflicting views between consumerists and professionals about standards for giving information are likely to continue for a long time. At the moment, consumers' widespread dissatisfaction with what they are given suggests that consumerists' standards are nearer consumers' interests than are professional standards.

CONTROL

. . . the most fundamental component in individual and social life is that of
control . . . the individual, either on his own or in coalition with others,
attempts to control the situation by controlling the behaviour of others as
well as his own, thus making control the most important dynamic of social
as well as of individual life.

Paul Sites (1973)[1]

INTRODUCTION

People can usually only control other people by influence, through
interactions in which the others accept the first's wish or will. That
acceptance may be glad or reluctant. But whoever's will prevails in
any encounter or situation can be said to control it.

Doctors and nurses expect to exercise control over the environment in which they work, over each other in complex ways, and
over patients. There are good reasons why they should. They have
statutory obligations and heavy responsibilities. There are also
more contentious reasons to do with interests and power. Some
control is necessary for professionals' management of themselves,
of their work and of their therapeutic tasks. Too little control by
them over their environment, each other and patients means that
treatment and care fail to be reliably provided at the right times. (It
does not mean chaos, as some hospital staff fear, because 'normal'
social controls continue to operate in most social situations,
wherever there are people. But Christmas in hospital can show
partial breakdown of treatment and care, when patients are
shuttled from one ward to another or drugs rounds are late.) On the
other hand, too much control by staff over patients or over other
staff moves reasonable control towards coercion or oppression.

Patients reciprocally expect and wish practitioners to guide and
instruct them. They comply on the whole with that guidance. But

patients expect to have some control themselves: it is necessary to their tasks of managing themselves, their illness and practitioners' work upon them. There is evidence that depriving patients of control reduces their psychological and physical wellbeing: if they are old or frail or immunologically impaired, reducing their control can decrease the length of their lives or hasten their deaths.[2] Extreme cases alert us to the probability that too little control may have deleterious effects on most patients, though those effects may be difficult to demonstrate. Conversely, benefits should be expected from giving patients greater control over some aspects of their treatment and care, and over the social and physical environment in which it is provided.

Part of practitioners' power to control patients is cast on them by patients' dependency and by their fear, conscious and unconscious, of practitioners' retaliation if crossed, challenged or criticized. Psychoanalytic theory holds that even healthy people fear that doctors and nurses will take revenge for bad thoughts by using their powers of life and death over them, when the chance comes.[3] In reality, staff do sometimes behave harshly or negligently towards 'unpopular' or 'difficult' patients. Nurses may delay handing them their post or forget to offer them a second piece of cake or go near them as little as possible.[4] Of course some patients are disagreeable people at the best of times. And sometimes staff are hardly aware of giving these petty punishments for patients' non-submission to staff's control or expectations. More seriously, elderly patients are especially likely to be punished through privations of one sort of another for non-compliance with medical and nursing regimes.[5] This can happen even in satisfactory wards and hospitals or in the community. The patients who do not comply are often the most independent ones. From their point of view, the care they receive does not match their expectations of responsiveness. They are striving to get staff to comply with their needs for pain relief, information, predictability and respect. So there can be 'a power struggle regarding who [is] in control and whether the patient [will] be allowed to maintain his independence in a dependent role'.[6]

Patients who manage to keep their fear of staff within rational bounds (and this is part of patients' task of managing their feelings) or who are relatively able and could leave hospital, often comply with staff's minor requirements, even if distasteful. They are then in a better position to evade or defy more significant demands. They note which nurses are flexible or rigid in their interpretation of rules and routines. They wait for the 'kind' ones. They learn how to handle staff. Describing a problem ('I feel sick') is usually a more effective way of getting help than offering a solution ('Please bring me a bowl' or 'May I have an anti-emetic?'). Non-verbal communication and the creation of an impression of status, worth or amiability are important. So are information and support from other patients. Staff know this, and can be at pains to prevent patients or relatives from comparing notes with each other.[7] Or staff lay stress on everyone's treatment regime being different, even when they are evidently the same.

These half-hidden struggles between staff and patients can be comic in narration afterwards. But they are distressing while they take place. Ideally, the boundary between control by staff and control by patients over any issue can be settled by negotiation. Sometimes it can be collective negotiation. The Patients Councils and Patients Participation Groups mentioned in Chapter 3 are perhaps better seen as negotiating bodies than as creators of new consumer standards for care and treatment. More often, negotiation is one-to-one between a patient or relative and a member of staff. But negotiation is seldom easy either for patients or for staff. Most lack experience of how to do it in a health-care setting where positions of relative disadvantage and advantage are so clear. Anger quickly surfaces on both sides. Giving more control to patients through institutionalized means, that are then subject to policies and standards, may be better from patients' point of view. They may be better, too, from staff's, at least for some issues.

Shifting control towards patients can be done in three main ways. Patients can be given direct control over some aspects of care or treatment, while they are in a health-care setting. (They have it anyway, when they are not. That is why many sick people find care at home preferable.) Patients can be given some way of exercising indirect control over staff's work in care or treatment. Or patients' control can be increased by increasing staff's responsiveness to patients' requests. We shall look at these in turn.

SHIFTING CONTROL

Direct control by patients over treatment or care

The body is a work-object for patients as well as for staff; given appropriate technology patients can work on it. A simple practice that gives some direct control over their treatment to patients in hospital is the self-administration of medications. Until a few years ago, even sleeping pills were compulsory on some wards. (Tactics for hiding and disposing of them were part of patient lore.) Nowadays sedatives and painkillers are usually offered at drug rounds and can be refused. But prescribed medicines are often still administered by nurses. Self-administration changes this:[8]

■ Patients are given several days' supply of medications to keep, usually in their bedside lockers. Their control is not complete; nurses have a statutory duty to ensure the safe and proper administration of medications, and from time to time they check how patients are doing. But the practice comes near enough giving independence to patients to provoke resistance. One consultant refused to allow her patients to join others in a scheme, as 'she felt she would no longer be in control'.

The therapeutic benefits of this practice should be the same as those for staff-administered medication; the medication is taken and has whatever effects it would have had. There are, however, other benefits: more communication from nurse to patient; clearer understanding of the medication's purposes; greater likelihood that patients will finish the course when they return home:[9]

■ A second example is patient-controlled analgesia, PCA. The self-administration of analgesic gas–air in childbirth has a long history. But PCA has only recently begun to be widely introduced for severe post-operative pain. In PCA, patients control the release of an analgesic infusion into the bloodstream by pressing a button on a small electronic pump that delivers the infusion through a narrow tube into a vein. Patients 'titrate' the analgesic against their pain, so using neither more nor less than is necessary. They can give themselves smaller and more frequent doses than is usual with analgesia injected at routine intervals by nurses. So the pain can be prevented from becoming intense. The pump allows only a pre-set maximum dose to be delivered cumulatively over a given time, to reduce the risk of patients overdosing themselves.

PCA has been pioneered by anaesthetists, and is increasingly used to control post-operative pain in children and adults. It can also be used in childbirth,[10] or modified as patient-controlled epidural anaesthesia.[11] The Royal Colleges' report *Pain after Surgery* (1990)[12] discusses, with remarkable frankness, outmoded professional beliefs about pain relief that prevent practitioners from giving adequate help to patients. Those beliefs are: that it is the doctor or nurse who is the authority on the patient's pain, not the patient; that the same causes of pain produce pain of the same

Table 8.1   Patient-controlled analgesia*

Patient's views	Nurses' views
'like idea of being in control'	no demands from patients, no
no hassle with nurses or need to	hassle
bother them	no worries about safety – safety
less pain, anxiety and discomfort	ensured by pre-set dose
greater satisfaction	

* The therapeutic benefits are less analgesic is used, there is less iatrogenic risk and a
  quicker recovery. Other benefits are a fuller explanation and better understanding
  between nurses and patients.

severity, and that equal doses of analgesics produce equal pain
control; that physical signs can be used to verify the existence of
pain and its severity, independently of what the patient says; and
that post-operative pain is unpreventable. These beliefs account for
many patients' experiences of being given pain relief too little, too
late or with scepticism instead of sympathy. (The narratives
described in Chapter 3 commonly make despairing and angry
comments about pain relief, especially about staff's disbelief of
what the narrators tell them.)

All effective pain relief has marked therapeutic benefits over
ineffective relief. It helps speed the restoration of major organ
systems' functioning, and so reduces the risk of serious post-
operative complications, because patients are not afraid to move or
breath deeply. So patients feel better and less stressed. But PCA
has further benefits over even promptly injected intramuscualr
analgesia. Patients need less analgesic; in one study of children after
orthopaedic surgery the dosage of opioid was halved.[13] They are
discharged earlier from hospital. And they feel less anxiety and
discomfort. PCA's benefits are summarized in Table 8.1.

In some other countries patients in hospital take responsibility for
more treatments than is usual in the UK. They include changing
bandages, recording fluid balance and monitoring intravenous
infusions.[14] Such self-care probably enhances safety. But it only
gives control to patients if it is carried out when the patients thinks
necessary or convenient. Then it meets that purpose.

From a professional viewpoint, these practices are to a higher
standard than the practices they replace because of their therapeutic advantages. (They are, of course, not to a higher standard if

patients are too unwell to nurse themselves, or if patients are deprived of nurses' company or other aspects of nursing care.) From a consumerist perspective, they are to a higher standard because, in addition to their therapeutic benefits, they enhance patients' freedom to act in their own interests.

Control over professionals' work

Patients' task of managing professionals' work on them is inevitably problematic, except when heteronomy and dependence are the chosen strategies. Practices that increase patients' knowledge of what is going on, and allow their surveillance of staff, help patients who wish to exercise autonomous management. They potentially enable them to exert some influence over what staff do, even though most patients are probably satisfied with inconspicuous observation. At the same time, such practices enhance patients' control over the management of themselves, their feelings and their sickness. Often the two cannot be separated. Practices that enable patients to remain conscious when they might have been unconscious are examples. Thus regional instead of general anaesthetisa lets the patient check which surgeon is doing the operation. But it also lets the patient replace the black hole of experience not experienced with knowledge. Epidural anaesthesia for caesarian section permits similar scrutiny of who is doing what, though most mothers' main reason for wanting it is to be conscious at their babies' births.

Again, standards that enable relations to stay with patients when the latter are unable to exert control themselves, have the same consequences. Thus a parent's presence during the induction of anaesthesia supports the child by comforting him or her. But it also protects the child from inappropriate remarks by staff. If such comments cannot always be prevented they can at least be interpreted by parent to child.

■ 'It's murder in there,' said one nurse to another, as mother and child waited outside theatre.[15]

Slapping and shouting at women in labour have vanished under the presence of fathers and other companions at childbirth. It is often said that patients' expectations are higher or staff's training better nowadays. Those may be so; but some improvements in care

are due to re-introducing 'ordinary' social controls into health-care settings.

This dual element in control, its enabling of patients' positive work on and for themselves and its constraining or negative effect on practitioners, makes many professionals feel ambivalent. They recognize the potential benefits to patients and the potential detriments to themselves. Thus controversy has been long and keen over the question of patients' access to the medical records about themselves.

After pressure from the National Council for Civil Liberties, the Freedom of Information Campaign, the Patients Association, MIND, Health Rights, the Consumers' Association, ACHCEW and some of the Royal Colleges, the Government passed two bills that gave patients access to their medical records. The Data Protection Act 1984 gave patients access to computer-held records from 1987. The Access to Health Records Act 1990 gave access to written records from 1991. Access means the right to read the records on request, subject to some limitations, against which patients can appeal.

These Acts were preceded by a number of schemes that voluntarily gave some patients access to their notes, either to read at their GP's surgery or to carry. These exceptional schemes have one thing in common. They are usually more popular with patients than with practitioners. Many practitioners 'don't see the point' or oppose them. When one group of people does not see the point of something that the other group sees very well, it is futile to question the former's sincerity or intelligence. Rather the not-seeing is a sign that the repression of the second group's interests is strong. Examples of the conflict are therefore instructive.

■ In a randomized controlled trial at St Thomas' Hospital, London, involving 246 women receiving antenatal care, both the group holding their notes and the control group wanted to have their own notes in future.[16] No notes were lost by the women, in spite of staff's prediction that they would be. But 26 per cent were said to be mislaid or lost in the hospital's custody – and some had tea spilt on them. For one woman, the loss was serious; she could not be given analgesics in labour until the hospital found her notes. 'Health professionals, almost without exception, believed that mothers liked having their own notes but not all of them felt that this was a reason for allowing mothers to have them.' In spite of this, the scheme has been extended to all pregnant women. But another trial, in West Berkshire, where women held their full obstetric notes as well as their antenatal notes, had to be abandoned before it could be evaluated, staff disliked it so much.[17]

■ In a pilot scheme in South London, all 51 severely mentally ill patients in the community, receiving care shared between their GPs, psychiatrists and community psychiatric nurses, were pleased to hold their records. 'Even patients who were very deluded were still able to use and value their shared care record . . .' Patients' enthusiasm far exceeded that of psychiatrists, GPs, nurses or managers, 'many of whom refused to cooperate with the scheme'.[18]

■ In another trial, at the Homerton Hospital, London, most of 50 rheumatology patients found being given a copy of the specialist's letter to their GPs helpful. (The sample who were given the letters found them as useful as did the control sample, who were offered an explanatory talk with paramedical staff after the consultation.) The patients expressed pleasure at being given copies of the letters. Their views were not shared by their GPs, some of whom felt it 'was inappropriate for patients to see the letters'.[19]

These examples show major differences in interests between patients and practitioners. The issues are usually presented as debates about who owns the information and whether reading their notes does patients good or harm. There is a split over ownership:

■ 'I'm proud of my case notes. It's like painting a picture. I don't want one of the figures in the picture to step out and maybe say "I don't like the way you've painted that house".'

Consultant obstetrician (1986)[20]

■ 'personal information should be redefined as belonging to the [patient], who . . . has a right to see, amend and record disagreement with anything kept on file or computer.'

View of users of mental illness services (1991)[21]

The second issue, whether reading the notes harms the patient, may seem more complex. But no-one proposes that patients who do not wish to read their notes should be made to do so. Those who choose to read them make an autonomous choice, with any consequences that follow from that. From the point of view of patients who want to manage their health and sickness and practitioners' work on and for them, the advantages of having access to records are many. Reading the records acts as an *aide-mémoire*; enables patients to point out errors or to dispute interpretations; inhibits doctors from writing down derogatory opinions about patients; helps patients check that the doctor has told the truth; and lets patients satisfy themselves that there have been no delays in diagnosis. If, in addition, the patient holds the records, or photocopies or print outs, and any X-ray films and records of exposure to radiation, there are further potential advantages. Patients can show them to other practitioners who become involved in the patient's care but who do not hold (or cannot gain immediate access to) the records. Duplicate or too frequent X-rays can be avoided; harmful interactions between drugs prevented; a quick understanding of the patient's health problems gained; and delays while records are sought eliminated.

Thus holding records potentially increases patients' safety. It increases their knowledge of themselves. It helps them understand their doctor's view of their sickness or condition. It makes it easier for them to find out more about their disease or the implications of their disability. It probably increases their compliance with the doctor's advice or leads them to challenge it openly. It should help them enter into constructive consultation with their doctor or nurse. It is difficult to say whether it makes for a more or less trusting relationship. But it must increase trust in those patients who suspect that there might be errors or snide comments in the record or that their doctor might not tell them the truth. In a study of 219 patients who had access to their GPs' records in an inner-city practice in Birmingham, 7.5 per cent gave, as a reason for reading them, 'to see if they had been told the truth'.[22] So it was a significant concern.

There is no systematic empirical evidence of benefits in outcomes to patients who have had full access to their records. The randomized controlled trial at St Thomas' showed no differences in the clinical states of mothers or their babies at birth. But samples in maternity care need to be very large to show small beneficial effects, and the control group of women had some, uncontrolled, access to their notes as they waited in ante-natal clinics – that is, some read them anyway. The women who carried their notes, however, attended ante-natal clinics more regularly than the controls, and reported that seeing their notes reduced their anxiety.[23]

Increasing staff's responsiveness to patients' requests

Asking for something is a patient's simplest way of trying to control staff's work with or on or for the self. Staff usually comply willingly with small, everyday requests – hence patients' common comments on staff's kindness. But more significant requests may fare less well.

Sometimes patients ask for something that staff think harmful. Agreement then is professionally unethical. Requests for cae-sarian section when there are no clinical reasons for it; for anti-biotics for viral diseases; for tranquilizers after bereavement, are examples. (Yesterday's professional practice can become today's lay demand.) But sometimes the presumption made by staff that they know best can conflict with patients' feelings or with their knowledge. Then patients have to bear the consequences of re-fusal of their requests; and they may be anguishing.

■ Up till 20 years or so ago women who asked to see their stillborn babies were usually refused. To save them pain was the reason, a reason blended with midwives' unacknowledged wish to save themselves pain. As some women protested and made the issue public, others who had not found a voice before, talked about their own unresolved grief over the babies they had not been allowed to see. The Stillbirth Society, a self-help and pressure group, was founded in 1978. Professional practice changed fairly quickly after that, and can be attributed largely to the society's work.[24] Parents were encouraged to see their babies. Photo-graphs were taken for parents to have later on, if they did not want them immediately. In 1991, the Society published a second edition of guidelines, written in consultation with lay and professional people, and including miscarriage.[25] Handling the foetus' body with respect; helping parents see and hold it; taking photographs and keepsakes; letting other children and grandparents see and hold the baby; perhaps taking him or her home; proper cremation or burial are the themes of this publication. The change in status of a dead foetus from a thing to be thrown away to a person to be known, however briefly, and loved, is remarkable and moving. It is a credit to the sensitivity of the professionals, as well as to the parents, who have helped to bring it about. But it poignantly illustrates the pity of not complying with patients' requests when they are first made.

Some other examples of refusals of patients' or relatives' requests, and of the pain and demonstrable detriments they can cause, were discussed in Chapter 6. The idea of responsiveness is new to discussions of standards in the health service. The increased control over staff by patients that it seems to imply makes it problematic. But oppressed interests are seldom trivial. Denial of them can constitute the opposite of kindness – unthinking cruelty.

9

CHOICE

It is clear to me that the treatment that is right for any individual patient is the treatment that the patient perceives as being the correct one.
J.M. Dixon, Consultant Surgeon in a unit that offers choice of treatment (1991)[1]

INTRODUCTION

Choice is a preference made from two or more things, present or proposed. The choices people make both express and define them: people act upon themselves and upon the world through their choices. Most people are continually making choices, whose consequences may be important or slight, foreseen or unpredictable. Even premature babies or very frail or almost unconscious people can indicate their preferences. The lives of us all are the product of the choices we have made and the necessities forced on us by chance and others' design. When disease, infirmity or incapacity come to people, the choices that they can still make assume special significance. Those choices retain in reality, and in symbol, power and control over some aspects of life, as well as expressing and defining the self. The more serious and restrictive the situations people find themselves in, the greater the importance of choice. Grave, life-threatening or intractable sickness, or sickness in harsh or confusing settings, can be said to put people into serious, even dire, situations. Making choices can then help stave off feelings of powerlessness and depression or apathy.[2]

To these existential reasons for offering choice to patients can be added pragmatic ones. People know their own circumstances, values and priorities best. Ideally they can choose their practitioner, treatment setting and treatment in the light of their knowledge of themselves. Doing that, they are more likely to feel comfortable

Table 9.1 Comparable standards for choice for elderly people in institutional care

Professional standards*	Consumerist standards**
Elderly patients should have:	*Old people in care should have*
free visiting throughout the day	*freedom to choose:*
opportunities for activities	when to see visitors
wishes and preferences about TV and radio respected	their own habits and lifestyles, own daily routine
a good choice of food	when to eat, sleep and wake
privacy must be preserved	to be private
should be able to visit other wards and outside the hospital	to be able to go out
own clothes	what to wear
own money, for choice, and for sense of security	to handle their own money
own patterns of bathing and washing, privacy for washing and bathing and elimination of waste products	to decide their own washing habits
	to wash, bath or use the toilet in private
be called by their own names	how to be addressed

* Taken from British Geriatrics Society and Royal College of Nursing (1975) *Improving Geriatric Care in Hospital*
** Taken from Age Concern (1991) *Basic Principles for Working with Older People who Need Care.*

and satisfied with what they have chosen, more likely to persevere with it. 'Ownership' of what is done, often considered so essential for professionals, applies to consumers, too.

Then there is intuition. What we call intuition is probably the rapid and complex evaluation of a multitude of factors, some external, some via the autonomic and central nervous systems, and based on previous experiences, remembered or forgotten, that produces an immediate conviction about some issue, question or problem. It is at least a reasonable hypothesis that the choices people make intuitively may be right for them therapeutically.

There are two provisos to these points. One is that before people can make wise choices, they must be adequately informed about the factors that are important to them. The other is that hope of cure may make people choose treatments that are more severe or more bizarre than they might have thought beforehand would be tolerable.[3] Choice is modified by actual situations.

Professionals and consumerists agree that choice for consumers is desirable. Sets of standards compiled by either often contain the word choice, or imply it. Table 9.1 gives an example for the care of the elderly. But there can be differences in the priority given to choice – shortages of staff or money may make choice seem a luxury to professionals (and corporate rationalizers) while to consumerists it remains a basic standard. There can be disagreement over what sort of issues lend themselves to choice. Semolina versus sago is easy. Choices that impinge on professional working practices or values are difficult. Then there are problems over the amount of information that patients and prospective patients should be given to help them make choices. Information and choice are readily confounded: there can be information without choice but there cannot be choice without information. Where practitioners are reluctant to give choice, for whatever reason, they incline to give little information. Where they are disinclined to give information, they avoid offering choice.

AREAS FOR CHOICE

Choice of practitioner – doctors

Everyone is free to choose a GP, and GPs are free to accept or refuse particular patients. Either can end the relationship at any time. These rights and opportunities safeguard the doctor–patient relationship as one of mutual choice as a basis for mutual confidence.

■ Although doctors are forbidden by their professional bodies to advertise, some practices offer more information to patients and prospective patients than others. Part of the 'manifesto' of a practice in Newcastle upon Tyne is reprinted as Table 9.2. There are 44 standards in the full document, though they can cover only a fraction of primary health care.[4] Some of the standards are statutory requirements; others are markers of excellent practice; a few are controversial in that other practitioners or consumer pressure groups might consider them too low. But as information that could help prospective patients choose between this and other practices, it sets a remarkably high standard.

Hospital specialists are technically consultants to GPs, not to patients. Many corporate rationalizers (probably all, though they may not choose to say so) would like to have access to information

Table 9.2   Extract from a primary health care team manifesto, Adelaide Medical Centre, Newcastle upon Tyne

---

Health promotion and preventive care

1   All children (whose parents have given consent) will be fully immunized.
2   All children will be screened at the appropriate intervals for treatable undetected conditions.
3   All adults aged 20–75 years will be screened opportunistically for hypertension every five years.
4   All adults aged 20–65 years will be offered a health check for coronary heart disease risk factors, and appropriate advice on lifestyle changes every five years.
5   All patients aged over 75 years will be functionally assessed annually.
6   Travellers abroad will be given appropriate advice and immunization.

Chronic care

1   Each diabetic patient will have a complete check annually.
2   Each hypertensive patient, once stable, will be reviewed six monthly.
3   Each patient on thyroxine will be monitored by blood test annually.

Terminal care

1   Any patient with terminal illness who wishes to die at home will be cared for by the team.
2   Bereaved relatives will be visited soon after a death.

---

about individual consultants' clinical interests and activities, including their rates for undertaking various procedures, and the mortality and morbidity associated with those rates. Many consumerists (and they do say so) would like that information to be made accessible direct to consumers. As the health service reforms take effect, it will be interesting to see how first GPs', then consumers', access to data on medical audit will affect choices of consultant.

Choice of midwife and nurse

Consumerists point out that women in labour in hospital can ask for another midwife if they do not like the one attending them, and that such requests should normally be met.[5] Choice of nurse is seldom suggested. That perhaps reflects the profession's own belief in the past in the interchangeability of nurses and its toleration of the fragmented care that results from that belief. But primary nursing, where one nurse takes total responsibility for the nursing care of a small group of patients from their admission to their discharge, is modifying that almost militaristic idea of interchangeability. Where primary nursing works well, patients are told of their right to change their primary nurse.[6] That is a step forward for patients and for nursing; a profession can only become a humane one when it recognizes its members' and its consumers' individualities.

Choice of case manager

People with long-term mental illness living in the community, that is, at home or in lodgings or hostels, are increasingly allocated a care or case worker or manager. A client's worker coordinates services needed by him or her, formulating a multidisciplinary care plan, coordinating a 'package' of care in accordance with that plan and monitoring the delivery and outcome of that care.

Some consumer pressure groups believe that the choice of case worker should be the consumer's.[7] Managers are more likely to allocate a worker, and change him or her if the relationship breaks down, than to give consumers choice amongst workers in the first place.

Choice of setting

The settings in which treatment and care can be given are various, even for some kinds of highly technical care. There is therefore often a potential choice of setting, though it may be constrained by lack of resources. Prospective consumers usually need information about both the range of choice and about the criteria for making one choice rather than another. But sometimes the information can be 'ordinary' – something they know already.

■ Of 84 terminally ill patients, 58 per cent wished to die at home; 20 per cent in hospital; and 20 per cent in a hospice, given existing circumstances.[8] Given ideal circumstances, the proportion of patients preferring to die at home went up. As it was, more died in hospital than had wished to.

A few CHCs have published guides to the choices of setting within their districts, and the pros and cons of each setting.

■ City and Hackney CHC's *Pregnancy and Birth in Hackney and the City of London*, published in 1986 and rewritten in 1989, lists the choices for antenatal care: nine community clinics (with the names of the consultant obstetricians who attend them); Homerton Hospital; or 'shared care' between the hospital and a GP.[9] The pros and cons of each are discussed. Then the pamphlet lists the four choices of where to have the baby: at home; in Homerton Hospital with delivery by a GP; in the consultant unit of Homerton Hospital; or at another hospital in London. It compares the advantages and disadvantages of each. The guide describes policies for various aspects of the service and their differences in the different settings. It indicates where difficulties in staff's attitudes or in the organization of the service may be encountered and how to overcome them. ('Sometimes this takes a bit of determination.' 'You may have to be assertive to get the kind of midwife you want.') It has a section on 'How to get a Home Birth or GP Delivery'. It describes the labour and delivery rooms in the hospital, and the post-natal ward. The pros and cons of the common obstetric procedures and drugs that may be met in a hospital delivery are discussed. How to choose from the procedures on offer in the hospital and how to fill in and use the 'birth plan' are described. The preface says:[10]

> The choices available to you may seem bewildering. Some decisions have to be made early on in your pregnancy – but you can still change your mind later on. Sometimes your midwife or doctor may recommend a change in your plans because of the way your pregnancy is progressing, and you and your carers may disagree on the best course of action. This Guide sets out to provide you with the information which will enable you to be clear about your options.

The booklet's author, Jessica James, met local obstetricians and midwives when writing it. The professionals felt doubt about the booklet's telling women how to ask for or refuse tests and treatments; how to choose a health-care setting; and what were the side effects of various treatments and drugs used in labour. But they were comfortable with the booklet's descriptions of clinical interventions and the reasons for them.[11] So information for acceptance or informed consent was more congenial to these professionals than information for informed choice.[12]

The choice of the setting for confinement is of special importance in the conflicts between some consumerists and many professionals. The choice between childbirth at home and in hospital has been kept alive by AIMS, NCT and a single-issue pressure group, the Society to Support Home Confinements. As well as the value these groups set on choice itself, they believe home confinements are safer for most births. Freedom from the stress and anxiety in hospital environments; the lack of technology to tempt staff into routine interventions; continuity of care from one or two midwives at home; the woman's greater control over her surroundings and the people in it; and perhaps choice itself, are believed by those groups to help labour progress more easily. There is some statistical evidence and interpretation to support this view, notably in Marjorie Tew's work.[13] The arguments are clouded by the differences in power that place confers upon women, midwives and obstetricians. Births at home give control and convenience to women. Births in hospital give control and convenience to obstetricians. Midwives are divided in their preferences. Corporate rationalizers are inclined to think that, though the consumer pressure groups are probably right, to change the service back to offering home confinements freely would be too troublesome and expensive: dominant interest-holders would not consent.[14] But the Royal College of Midwives is beginning to think otherwise.[15] So those changes may find support, if the midwives make alliances with local corporate rationalizers – specialists in public health and managers drawing up specifications for providing and purchasing maternity services.

Choice of hospital

Hospitals and wards within hospitals vary. Their clinical and non-clinical policies, facilities, routines and 'atmosphere' reflect the views and wishes of their current staff and managers and the institutionalized philosophies and preferences of past staff. Individual patients' wishes and perceptions of their own needs may count for little. Choice of hospital or ward therefore is important to consumers, as indeed it is to staff seeking some ways of working rather than others.

Some consumer pressure and self-help groups build up knowledge of hospitals and give advice to people who ask for it. But they seldom publish comparative information, partly from lack of resources, partly from fear of antagonizing professionals by naming 'bad' hospitals. There is thus an underworld of information accessible to some potential consumers but not to others.

■ In the 1970s some parents on the outskirts of London took their children to inner-city teaching hospitals for elective surgery, because visiting was unrestricted there and restricted in the local hospitals. The NAWCH network helped them with the choice.

■ Occasionally CHCs have asked GPs not to refer patients to named hospitals where standards are especially low. CHCs tried to get wards for ENT surgery for children in Bradford (Yorkshire) and in Bromley (South London) boycotted because of their policies of very restricted access by children to their parents. CHCs thus in effect asked GPs to make the choice that well-informed parents would make for themselves.

These examples illustrate the difficulties of disseminating information for choice to 'ordinary' consumers. The only major national comparative source of information, freely available and written from a consumerist perspective, has been *The Good Birth Guide*.[16] Published in 1979 by Sheila Kitzinger, an adviser to NCT, the paperback book contained descriptions of policies and staff's attitudes in 229 named maternity units in England, Scotland and Wales. The descriptions were based on 1759 letters from women who had had babies from 1976 to 1977. In addition, the senior nursing officers of the units (directors of midwifery services) were asked about their units, though some declined to answer.

The book stated the author's values and criteria for a good birth, and had brief definitions and discussion of obstetric terms and procedures. The descriptions would have allowed readers to judge the units' approaches towards induction, acceleration of labour, foetal monitoring and other interventions; and policies about contact between mother and baby, feeding, visitors and other non-clinical matters. These accounts from inside were important because practitioners tend to believe that they give individual care, according to patients' needs, without taking into account the non-negotiable routines that form the context of that care.

Not all the maternity units in the country were covered. And units can change for better or worse quickly, with the arrival of a new consultant or sister. But anyone reading the book would have been helped to think about her own preferences and where they were most likely to be met. Maternity care staff, too, could have seen what mattered to consumers. Though there was a wide range of practices across the country, patterns of care in any one unit tended to be limited. Disregard of current government guidance on standards was often evident. Three hospitals, the West London in Hammersmith, St Mary's in Manchester, and the John Radcliffe in Oxford,[17]

were given special mention as places where freedom of choice and respect for the individual is linked with human caring; where one's partner is given a warm welcome, there is opportunity for full discussion concerning medical procedures, support for coping in labour in whatever way one wishes, and where it is accepted that the baby belongs to the parents and is not the property of the hospital.

The *Guide* has not been recently updated or reprinted. But it was a model of its kind.

There is more published comparative work on standards in USA than in this country.

■ The Public Citizen Health Research Group has published rankings of mammographic screening facilities in Washington, DC.[18] It scored them for their answers to a questionnaire covering volume of work done; information to patients (including whether patients were informed of the risks of mammography and whether they were sent reports of their mammograms' results); physical examination of patients; staff's training; equipment and procedures; and quality control, paying special attention to the dose of radiation per image. Eleven facilities were put in rank order; those that did not reply were not ranked (that is, women were tacitly advised to avoid them). The report also included a discussion of screening, of risk factors for breast cancer and of recommended intervals for screening. Again, it is a model of its kind, giving women information from which to make choices about the style and safety of the services.

Both the Royal College of Radiologists and the Consumers' Association have published data showing that, as in the study above, some X-ray departments use higher doses of radiation than are necessary. But neither named the departments.[19,20]

The specification for service agreements between providers and purchasers will spell out some of the standards for care and treatment adopted within provider hospitals and community units. These should in time provide comparative information to the public. But consumerists will always want to see information given in greater detail than managers will. So the need for information, collected and made available by consumerists, will remain.

Choice of treatment

Choices of treatment for minor health problems are made every day by patients in their GPs' surgeries – or choice of no treatment, when patients throw away a prescription from a therapeutic conviction of their own. The opportunity for choice of treatment for serious or difficult diseases or conditions is less common, for rather few have treatments of equal efficacy and roughly equal risks, costs and benefits. (Treatments of very different risks and outcomes are discussed in Chapter 10 on decision-making, for sometimes it is treatment itself rather than choice between treatments that is the issue.) Consumerists think that patients should be offered a choice of treatment where more than one appears to be clinically appropriate. But choice itself should not be enforced or even subject to persuasion; patients should be free to choose or reject choice. If they choose choice, they should be offered the information relevant to the choice, and in the detail they require to make it. If they prefer to make an 'intuitive' choice after the minimum relevant information, that too may be right for them. Controlling the amount of information coming in, and making choices in its light, are parts of patients' management task. Helping them do that is part of professionals' management task. That help can, and often should, include the practitioner's advice and the reasons for it. Their experience and preferences have an explicit place in the discourse between them and patients.

Professionals' views of choice are more complicated. They are trained to make decisions about treatment and (what is not the same thing) take responsibility for those decisions. But responsibility is a problematic concept when applied to a decision that someone else could have taken. Some professionals feel that their choices lift the burden of responsibility from their patients. But when outcomes, side effects or complications might be bad, some patients will feel that it is even more important that the choice at least should be theirs. Others will be more regretful and angry at the 'failure' of their choice than they would have been at the doctor's. (It will be worst of all when a patient's wishes or doubts are expressed before the choice and disregarded.) Some patients, too, positively prefer not to make choices of treatment ('You are the doctor') or cannot make them. So professionals' cautious view of patients' choice can seem justified in view of these uncertainties.

A second reason for some professionals' reluctance to offer choice is the Bluebeard syndrome – dread that a patient will unlock the door to knowledge and stumble on unbearable horrors. Some information is frightening. Some is uncertain and difficult to explain in terms of probabilities. Some is complex and difficult to understand. Distressing patients and diminishing therapeutic hope comes uneasily to practitioners. Moreover, there are probably rather low levels of general knowledge about common diseases and their treatments in this country. Even booklets written to give information to

Table 9.3   Content analysis of international literature on breast disorders (adapted from Goddard and Bowling, 1987)[21]

Topic*	UK	France	Sweden	USA
statistical incidence of breast cancer	+	+	+	+
risk factors	+	+	+	+
value of early detection	+	+	+	+
breast structure illustrated	−	+	+	+
description of different surgical treatments	−	+	+	+
description of radiotherapy	−	+	+	+
description of chemotherapy	−	+	+	+
side effects described	−	+	+	+
prognostic information given	−	+	+	+
metastasis mentioned	−	+	+	+
address of support agencies	+	+	+	+

* + = mentioned in at least one of the booklets; − = not mentioned.

the public tend to omit or play down unpleasant facts. Practitioners' task of giving information to patients, and patients' preparedness to ask questions, are both made more difficult by this 'cultural' reticence. Table 9.3 illustrates the point by its comparison of information about breast disease given in publications produced by health education and national cancer societies in four countries. Breast cancer is a common disease, with a high mortality rate, in the UK. Yet the UK literature 'lacked amplification' and was 'reassuring but not revealing' in not mentioning 'negative aspects of breast disease and its treatment'.[21]

A third reason for some professionals' reluctance to offer choice is their clinical conviction that some treatments are better than others, even though current evidence is that the outcomes are the same. Imperfect knowledge tends to sustain personal conviction quite as much as it diminishes it.

Related to this reason is technical preference. A doctor or other practitioner may like doing one sort of procedure more than another, and be more skilled at it. Then patients may be better off with the practitioner's choice. But that means that patients must know practitioners' preferences before they know the diagnosis; clearly a problem, though one that GPs can help solve through their knowledge of consultants' preferences and skills.

The last reason is to do with clinical acumen or intuition. Just as some patients can be supposed to have feelings about what would be right for them, so can some clinicians be supposed to have intuitions about what would be right for some individual patients. That is an argument for choices being made by practitioner and patient together, rather than by either alone.

These professional concerns, together with some consumers' inclination to heteronomy, have meant that the standard that choice should be offered has spread more slowly than consumerists would like. Clinical research that includes choice tends to look at what choices patients make, and at those treatments' psychological effects on patients, rather than at the effects of offering or not offering choice itself. And practitioners sometimes offer or allow choice, not as a good in itself but only because there is no evidence that one course of action is better or worse than another. Though that is a good reason for offering choice, it should not be the only one. Different values and the fallibility of medical knowledge make choice an ethical and a practical good. But both thinking and research about choice are at an early stage.

Conditions or procedures where choice can be offered, at least sometimes, include contraception; sterilization; renal failure (haemodialysis or peritoneal dialysis); thyrotoxicosis (surgery or radioactive iodine); cancer of the prostate (orchidectomy or hormone-blocking drugs); breast cancer. There are also choices within choices, like in-patient or day surgery; type of anaesthesia; type of drug.

The value of choice is best understood in treatment for early breast cancer. Mastectomy or local excision of the tumour plus radiotherapy have equal outcomes, as far as is known, in rates of survival, when combined with appropriate chemotherapy or hormone-blocking therapy. Some women who are invited to choose between treatments find it easy.[22] Others find it more difficult; but only a few regret afterwards having made a choice. There is some evidence (the numbers are small) that women who are not offered choice are more depressed and anxious after treatment than those who are.[23] A King's Fund Consensus Statement, made in 1986 by a panel of six experts and six lay people, included the standard that 'women should be involved in treatment decisions'.[24]

Some professionals pay more attention than others to that standard. In some units for breast disease, like that in Edinburgh, great care is taken to give women information about options and to avoid influencing their choices by any unconscious biases staff may have.[25] But a study in London could only draw on a small number of surgeons who regularly offered choice.[26] Nevertheless, the women who were treated by those surgeons suffered less anxiety and depression, even when, for clinical reasons, they were not offered choice than those treated by surgeons who never offered choice. This suggests that some difference in the amount of information, or discussion, or attitude of the surgeons, confounded choice. The women may have felt that the surgeons who usually offered choice, had discussed the possibilities and constraints about treatment so openly that, in spite of there being no choice, the decision was right for them.

There are comparable, though less extensive, findings for men with advanced cancer of the prostrate. They too make choices of treatment with which they are comfortable and that fit their priorities.[27] Longitudinal studies of choice have not been designed or implemented for long enough to provide data on lengths of survival. But our knowledge of psychobiological factors suggests that avoidable psychological morbidity is in general better avoided that courted. Social factors come in, too, as new standards spread. Once consumers know that choice is possible, some will feel angry that it was not discussed with them. That will be so whether or not they choose to make the choice.

10

DECISION-MAKING

... inadequacies and shortcomings ... are present within every course of human conduct.

Grant R. Gillett (1989)[1]

INTRODUCTION

Making a decision can be thought of as an internal monologue in which the self checks its observational, experiential and theoretical knowledge against its values and priorities in order to arrive at a course of action. Some monologues remain internal, when people make decisions on their own. In a clinical interview or encounter between two people, each internal monologue can be kept largely private or it can be put into a dialogue between them. To the extent that one contributes and influences the other, each participates in making decisions about the course of action that will be followed. Dominant interest-holders sometimes talk about 'patient participation' in decision-making. But that is misleading, just as it would be if repressed interest-holders talked about 'practitioner-participation'. Both patient and practitioner take part. Both have their own interests in finding a course of action that suits their purposes and concerns.

Practitioners are trained to make decisions for patients, and to put those decisions in the form of advice. Traditionally, patients' only formally recognized power in this decision-making has been the right to refuse any or all of the procedures or treatments advised. (This right comes from common law where any interference with another's person without his or her consent constitutes assault.) But the right of refusal only, though an important safeguard, has two disadvantages. It leaves other possible courses of action off the agenda, unless they have already been discussed and dismissed between practitioner and patient. And it is difficult to exercise openly without confrontation. The emphasis on giving advice rather than explanation has led practitioners (doctors, nurses and paramedics) to be more skilled at persuasion than at discussion, more dependent on authority than on rationale. And it has sometimes tempted them to take short cuts in gaining or assuming consent. Consumerists and medical ethicists have challenged the ethical basis of professional decisions that they have seen as too global, denying patients the opportunity to consent to or refuse each component procedure; as invalid, because inadequate information was given to patients beforehand; or as unethical, because patients knew nothing of them and could neither have consented nor refused. Greater sensitivity to these sorts of issues is leading to changes in how decisions are made. But both the greater power of practitioners compared with patients (even the energy and confidence that come from being well, not ill, contribute to the inequality of power) and also the doubts of both practitioners and patients about how much the latter want to share in decision-making, make the formulation of standards for good practice difficult. There is, above all, a lack of models of how patients can be brought into decision-making effectively and in a way that does not substitute concealed coercion for the traditional take-it-or-leave-it model of decision-making.

Nevertheless, there is the beginning of an acceptance amongst most practitioners that patients 'should make their own deliberated decisions within the context of their own life plans and preferences, so far as this does not harm others'.[2] Decision-making goes further than choice between alternatives with approximately the same outcomes. It includes more complex decisions where the outcomes may or will be different. There are three ways in which this kind of decision-making can be strengthened:

1 The range of decisions that patients take on their own, or largely on their own (for their internal monologues, without consultation with practitioners) can be extended by changes in professional and administrative practices.
2 Ways can be found for patients to contribute their voice, and even their decisions, beforehand to situations where later their capacity for contribution may be lessened.
3 The dialogue between patients and practitioners can be changed to enhance each's contribution to it.

Consumerists see patterns of provision and care that enable consumers to take their own decisions at a higher standard than those that prevent them. They see practices that establish patients' wishes and decisions in advance of the occasion to execute them as at a higher standard than those that leave practitioners to decide on their own. And they see encounters between practitioners and patients that foster openness and clarity between the two as at a higher standard than those in which patients' influence is minimal; or that contain patients' or practitioners' hidden agendas; or oppress or suppress patients' interests.

PATIENTS MAKING THEIR OWN DECISIONS

> There are many clinical situations in which the patient's statement of what he wants is exactly what he needs.
>
> Psychiatrist[3]

People living in the community are in the strongest position to make their own decisions. They are not obliged to enter the health-care system and can usually leave it again. How 'correctly' people refer themselves, with what clinical justification or therapeutic benefit, is difficult to say. Some patients delay until diagnosis and treatment come too late. But doctors too fail to heed in time patients' or relatives' disquiet or proferred diagnoses. Less momentously, it has been shown that when patients book an appointment with a GP, they can decide accurately how much time they will need for the consultation.[4] Giving them that, instead of allocating them standard appointments, uses everyone's time efficiently. This finding is only surprising because much of the routinization of health care conceals patients' ability to manage aspects of it themselves.

Self-referral to a GP can be extended to self-referral to walk-in clinics. This allows consumers to make their own decisions about seeking specialized advice or treatment. Family planning, well women, well men, baby, sexually transmitted diseases, psychiatric and stress clinics meet this purpose. In some clinics, patients decide which professional or other service they require, without a preliminary interview or the routine of progressing through a series of staff, from clerk to nurse to doctor.

■ In a Well Woman clinic in a socio-economically deprived part of Glasgow, women tick what service they want (nurse councillor, doctor, self-help group for a specific problem, general health discussion group) or what health checks (blood pressure, haemoglobin level, cervical smear, etc.).[5] Most women have taken to this, valuing the saving in time and the increased confidentiality. (It is likely they valued things more difficult to ask about in surveys, too, like the greater control over events, and the lack of 'processing'.) Some women found it difficult to make decisions rather than remain passive, however. That can be expected from the role of passive patients expected from them in the past and from the normal distribution of sorts of personality in any population.

■ A psychiatric walk-in clinic in Boston, Massachusetts, has gone further. Instead of offering a list of services, its psychiatrists led by Dr Lazare, invite patients to say what treatment or outcome they want from their visit.[6] Patients generally know what they want, though they sometimes need help in clarifying their request. If the request falls within professionally accepted practice and can be met from the clinic's resources, it is granted. If not, the psychiatrist and patient negotiate, discussing further possibilities. The patient evaluates and accepts or rejects the proposals. The psychiatrist offers more information about alternative diagnostic or treatment plans. The doctor is honest about the reasons for refusing requests, including lack of financial or appropriate clinical resources. (That contrasts with UK practice, where patients are generally told that they would not benefit clinically, rather than that something is not available or cannot be afforded for them. This may change, as professionals become more disaffected with the rationing of resources and public discussion of the problem increases.) Patients' requests, though varied (e.g. for a different psychotropic medication, for talking over their feelings after a stressful experience, for brief personal support) are usually modest and can be met: 'Patients do not want to be different human beings. They want to feel better.'

Dr Lazare and his colleagues call this the 'customer approach' to patienthood. The patient decides what to ask for and can take his or her business elsewhere if dissatisfied. The doctor listens. He or she can decide not to grant the patient's request, if it is clinically (or ethically) inappropriate. The process is based on mutual influence and negotiated consensus. The definition of what the patient needs does not rest solely with the practitioner.

The authors describe how practitioners and patients both tend at first to resist the customer approach: 'It is as if there were a conspiracy between both parties in which the patient agrees not to say what he wants and the clinician agrees not to ask.' Patients believe that stating their wishes openly will be taken as confrontational. They must only hint at them; the clinic is an adversary who may say no. Practitioners believe that they know best; or that patients can't say what they want; or that professional norms are let down by responding to patients' requests; or that authority for treatment would be relinquished; or that patients' wants ('demands') would be insatiable. But the authors believe that both practitioners and patients benefit from the customer approach. They believe it improves patient care, patient satisfaction and staff morale. In a second paper, it is reported that patients who had experienced the customer approach felt more satisfied and helped than those who had not.[7]

People with chronic sickness or disability are accustomed to making their own decisions when living in the community. They can become more adept than practitioners in interpreting how they feel and what action to take – more rest, more exercise, which medication.[8] If they read specialist medical and self-help publications, their theoretical as well as their pragmatic knowledge can outdistance that of generalist practitioners. Day-to-day decisions become their own, with professionals providing technical diagnostic services and information from time to time. Professional standards of care have to include sensitivity to this; they have to avoid infringement of patients' authority or sense of successful management of their situation.[9] A quotation from a narrative illustrates bad practice:[10]

■ The wife of a tetraplegic mentioned to two community nurses that she was married to a tetraplegic. 'I'm sorry, dear, you must have got it wrong. Looking after a tetraplegic is a skilled nursing task requiring two nurses, so you couldn't possibly do it by yourself.' [This comment was] not only extremely patronising . . . but it violated the direct experience that both my wife and I had.

Husband (1988)

DECIDING IN ADVANCE

Birth plans compiled by women during pregnancy are a good example of how decisions can be made in advance about treatment and care. They have been introduced into maternity care in the last 10 years or so, following some women's arrival in hospital in labour with their own plans. Some birth plans record women's choices from standard alternatives. Others are wider ranging and written in narrative form. They cover such issues as the use of foetal monitoring; analgesics; position in labour; presence of partner or friend; intensity of light in the room; episiotomy. The plan is kept in the woman's notes, or by her, or both. Unexpected events during labour may mean that a plan cannot be followed exactly. But its general tenor will indicate to practitioners the sort of experience of birth the woman would like to have.

At life's other end, the approach of death, advance directives record decisions about how people want to be cared for if no longer competent to discuss the matter, in critical illness, dementia, terminal illness or permanent unconsciousness. There are three kinds of advance directives: 'living wills'; discussion of possibilities and preferences with a doctor; or (in the USA) the appointment of someone with power of attorney to make decisions. The issues include removal from home to hospital, cardiothoracic resuscitation, intensive care, artificial ventilation, tube feeding and other life-support technologies. Cardiothoracic resuscitation is of particular interest because 'Do not resuscitate' is, in the UK, quite commonly written in elderly patients' notes without their knowledge or consent.[11] Indeed, it is even argued that they should not be asked, lest their wish to be resuscitated be 'inappropriate'.[12] Conversely, some patients are resuscitated who might have preferred not to be.

In USA, states began passing legislation to cover living wills in 1976. The federal Patients' Self-Determination Act 1990 requires all hospitals receiving Medicare or Medicaid funding to inform patients on admission of their right to make advance directives.[13]

■ A survey in 1988 in Boston, Massachusetts, showed that about 90 per cent of the general public in Boston and of out-patients at a teaching hospital were in favour of advance directives, though few had made them (about 9 per cent of the USA population in 1987).[14] Respondents felt that the initiative in raising the subject should come from their doctor. But they did not feel the subject was too sensitive to be raised.

■ A prospective study in North Carolina in 1987 encouraged elderly people to make advanced directives and later examined doctors' compliance with them.[15] 96 patients' recorded wishes were followed 75 per cent of the time. But care was more aggressive in six instances and less aggressive in 18 than had been requested. Some of the discrepancies were due to unforeseen contingencies for which the care given was clinically appropriate. But others were due to doctors or relatives overriding patients' wishes in order to reach a 'wise decision'.

An American organization, Concern for the Dying, has promoted the living will to the public and professionals since the early 1970s.[16] Doctors have been in the forefront of discussion and acceptance of it. It is probable that we shall only catch up with American policy in the UK when there has been sustained pressure from consumerists and proto-professionals. The Natural Death Centre, founded in 1991 in London, is working for the legal recognition of living wills, as part of its work to demystify death.[17]

Contemplating and recording decisions in advance will perhaps come to be seen as constituting an important aspect of the self's management of various serious or chronic progressive illnesses in their early stages. As long as the self is competent, decisions can be changed. Conflicts over the boundary between clinical exigency and clinicians' or patients' preferences are inevitable. But the discussion of such issues increases the sum of knowledge and sensitivity in health care.

ENHANCING THE CLARITY OF THE CLINICAL DIALOGUE

There are three kinds of decision-making: autonomous, shared and heteronomous. For complex clinical decisions, many proto-professionals and consumerists would regard shared decision-making as the ideal, though recognizing that some consumers would choose heteronomy. Research shows that consumers can make that choice:[18]

■ 69 per cent of patients with cancer in a hospital in Albany, New York, wanted to 'participate in decisions made about my medical care and treatment'. Almost all of the patients who wanted 'participation' wanted 'as much information as possible, good or bad'; less than 1 per cent wanted good news only; and none wanted only minimal information. By contrast, of the 31 per cent who wanted 'to leave decisions about my medical care and treatment up to my doctor', only 75 per cent wanted full information; 16 per cent wanted good news only; and almost 9 per cent wanted minimal information. (Nevertheless, 92 per cent of all patients wanted full information.) Younger patients and women wanted to share in decision-making more than older patients and men.

Younger people and women are probably more radical in matters of health care than older men. Women have more encounters with health care than men, through childbearing and the care of children. They are also more likely to be treated patronizingly by male doctors. Being patronized alerts people to the low regard in which they are held, and therefore to possible harm to their interests. At a different level of explanation, women have less to lose by opposing dominant interests than men (and younger people than older), because they are less likely to be accepted and rewarded by dominant interest-holders anyway.

But research also shows that patients' reluctance to choose shared decision-making may be due to specific negative factors.

■ In a study of 12 patients in hospital in Liverpool none wanted to take part in decisions about nursing care.[19] Some took an instrumental view of nurses' expertise as being greater than their own. But others' fear of antagonizing nurses by 'not toeing the line' came out in interviews. The practice on the wards was, in fact, not to involve patients in decision-making.[20]

In the clinical consultation, practitioners are practised in guiding and controlling the dialogue between themselves and patients. Those seeking their help expect guidance. But sociological research, as well as ordinary experience, shows that there can be problems. Patients' opportunities to disclose their concerns and to elicit the information they want can be constricted. And patients can be manipulated into agreeing to – even apparently choosing – the course of action the practitioner prefers. The first can oppress patients' interests, the second suppress them.

Practitioners and patients are often aware that constriction of patients' concerns takes place, though they may be unsure of how it happens or who is responsible for it. The constriction is usually attributed to lack of 'communication skills' in either or both.[21] Proto-professionals and consumerists advise patients to note what they want to say on a piece of paper before a consultation in the GP's surgery, in out-patients, or from a hospital bed. But some professionals resent the piece of paper.[22] This suggests that communication is not the issue. Rather there are complex plays of interest beneath the dialogue's surface. The practitioner wants to hear and say things synergistic with his or her interests and tries to manage the dialogue to that end. The patient may want to raise issues that conflict with those wants: non-medical problems; ethically troubling disclosures; trivial sicknesses; incoherent anxieties; imaginary symptoms; incurable conditions; pleas for sympathy and support. The patient's management task in striving to get his or her concerns accepted is difficult. Added to the conflicts of interest that can make the blocking of communication dominant interest-holders' unconscious aim, rather than its enhancement, there can be other problems. There are often differences in status and class, vocabulary, and knowledge of the structure of the discourse – the unwritten rules of clinical dialogue through which power is exerted. Those rules are familiar to practitioners but seldom to patients.[23] (Though they are reasonably familiar to practised patients, and especially in long-term relationships, as noted in Chapter 2.) The mutual dissatisfaction that can result during clinical interviews is a sign of interests oppressed; both parties feel resentment against the other.

Suppression of patients' interests is more difficult to identify; patients feel no suspicion or anger. They may feel, indeed, that a practitioner has done his or her best, giving sound advice and willing help. The example of withholding effective treatment for heart disease from elderly patients is an example (Chapter 1). Any institutional policies, or any practitioners' personal preferences, that discriminate against people in ways they are unaware of, suppresses their interests. Such suppression can be picked up by finding statistically significant differences in treatment between groups of patients who might be thought to be eligible for the same treatment. It can also be traced in individual consultations between one practitioner and a series of patients.

■ Women with abnormal smears from cervical cytology were more likely to be treated by hysterectomy than by cryosurgery or cone biopsy in a public-sector community clinic in California than in a private sector faculty clinic. The faculty clinic was staffed by senior doctors. The community clinic was staffed by junior doctors, who needed surgical experience during their training.[24]

■ In a paediatric cardiology clinic in London, a technically sophisticated centre taking referrals from all over the country, tests and procedures carried out on normal children with congenital heart disease were not offered to children with Down's syndrome. Whereas the risks of surgery were played down to parents of normal children, parents of Down's syndrome children were encouraged to see treatment and its complications as something that would interrupt their happy lives.[25] In the terms of Chapter 5, Down's children were not treated as work-objects and person-subjects, but as person-subjects only.

In these examples, the decision for any particular patient might have been right. What was lacking were complete sharing of information by the practitioner (including disclosure of his or her own interests) and full exploration of the patients' interests.

Hysterectomy is more traumatic and risky than the other treatments, as well as putting an end to child bearing. Leaving congenital heart disease untreated brings forward death. For children with Down's syndrome, that probably means dying before they reach their full potential.

Oppression and suppression of patients' interests within clinical dialogue and clinical decision-making are difficult to tackle. Recognizing that they can happen is the first step. The second step is a critical examination of all decision-making. In the USA, the President's Commission for the Study of Ethical Problems has reached an important stage in that examination. It has concluded that even when patients and practitioners have agreed that the patient should be heteronomous (called the 'authorative guidance model' of decision-making), the result may be questionable.[26] Patients may choose the model by default and play too little part in shaping the relationship. An active 'partnership and active participation' model is therefore to be preferred.

In the UK, we are less advanced in our thinking. But 'partnership' has come into the language of general practitioners,[27] and is likely to spread. What it means will have to be worked out. People use words long before they understand their meanings. They create meanings through their actions. But whatever partnership comes to mean, respect, support, information and control will sustain patients' part in it. The trend is set.

STANDARDS AND SPECIFICATIONS

Whatever our contrasts and differences we want to see things changed and improved.

Pensioners in Hackney, London,
about the community health services (1990)[1]

INTRODUCTION

The specifications for service agreements introduced by the Conservative Government into the NHS in 1991 are a new way of trying to secure high standards of treatment and care. It is important that those drawing them up have a strong sense of what 'improvement' means. The principles underlying trends in consumerist and proto-professional standards, and hence in due course in some professional standards, show what the trends in improvement are. (I say some professional standards, because many professional standards are synergistic with consumers' interests, whether apparent or inapparent.) We can tell 'higher' from 'lower', either by tracing the succession of values for a particular standard, or by going back to those principles.

■ In the 1940s, women having babies in hospital could only have the baby's father with them during visiting hours; in the 1950s, for the first stage of labour; in the 1960s, for the second stage (the birth) for normal deliveries as well; in the 1970s and 1980s, for some instrumental deliveries. In the 1990s, some hospitals still bar the father from some instrumental deliveries, in spite of requests and complaints. So high standards for support and for choice are not yet fully met.

In the first part of this chapter, I shall recapitulate the discussion so far, as it relates to trends. In the second, some of the problems that remain after a shared understanding of higher and lower is attained are discussed.

TRENDS IN STANDARDS

Standards express values. Values are derived from changing knowledge, increasing sensibility, shifts in power and new perceptions of interests. The direction in which consumerist general standards move is towards increasing consumers' freedom to act in their own interests (Chapter 3). Even when consumers cannot act in their own interests, consumerist standards protect their interests indirectly.

■ Open visiting benefits most obviously patients who are conscious but vulnerable – the very young, the elderly, the seriously sick. But it opens up hospitals to the presence, observation and influence of outsiders in ways that, though inconspicuous, can reassure and protect patients who have no visitors or who are weak, severely mentally ill, or unconscious.

■ Setting a high value on individually-chosen and agreed treatment and care safeguards the interests of those patients who can enter into clinical discussions. For those who cannot, or do not choose to, the emphasis on individual treatment will tend to help practitioners think carefully about what meets the interests of those patients as individuals. Moreover, emphasis on individual treatment is more likely than treatment by category to lead practitioners to challenge or disclose suppressed interests.

We have seen to what consumerist and proto-professional standards are broadly directed: to greater respect for consumers as work-objects and person-subjects; to unrestricted support from relations; to freely given and accurate information; to increased control, choice and decision-making. The fine detail and ramifications of what each of these may come in time to mean is to us as yet unknown. But in that lies the challenge and excitement of consumerist and professional work in the future.

Nevertheless, understanding these trends makes it possible to predict what will be the next stage of a standard for some specific issue or practice. It makes it easy to recognize when a new idea or a modification of an old one would constitute a higher standard. The number of standards in health care increases over time, as new issues, hitherto unnoticed, or regarded as non-problematic, are identified. Anselm Strauss' and Barney Glaser's book, *Anguish:*

Case History of a Dying Trajectory, shows how patients can experience care that is neglectful and unkind because some of its components are outside staff's professional remit and so not subject to defined standards.[2] But every new issue identified and made subject to standards needs to be scrutinized by consumerists as well as by professionals. What consumerists intend to be liberating, professionals may make compulsory. What are 'ordinary' acts of consideration may be turned into patronizing, intrusive or demeaning 'caring'.

■ Staff in paediatric wards put up stalwart resistance to parents for years, excluding or ignoring them (Chapter 6). The standard that they should be made welcome and encouraged to share in the care of their children is no longer controversial.[3] But there is a new professional standard:

  The nurse will monitor the physical and emotional well-being of resident parents.[4]

In effect that tries to convert autonomous adults, part of whose function is to protect their children from the impact of the hospital environment and from any ill-considered remarks and actions of the nurses, into patients. Except in instances of suspected non-accidental injury to children, it is the role of parents to 'monitor' (though the term lacks the respect that one person-subject ought to have for another) nurses, and not vice versa. As standards of treatment and care rise in number and complexity, so do risks of distortion of their purposes.

Trends in standards can be presented in various ways and some of these are shown in Table 11.1.[4] Some standards affect several aspects of care and treatment, so the same standard can be put under different headings. The same standard can also be put under different headings because low standards work with each other against patients' wellbeing and high standards work with each other for patients' wellbeing.

■ Lack of privacy, for example, can be used by staff to argue against open visiting for adults, against having parents in the post-operative recovery area, or against giving full information to some patients. The arguments may or may not be convincing. But they could not be put forward, were there better environmental standards of privacy.

So each high standard contributes on its own, and enhances the others.

Table 11.1   Trends in standards

From	To	Examples
Environmental care		
utilitarian	comfortable	carpets instead of vinyl flooring; easy chairs, not hard; curtains instead of bare windows
'clinical'	domestic	pictures, plants, large spaces divided into smaller areas for different activities
harsh	gentle	low rather than bright lights in SCBUs; noise levels kept down; attention to colour of walls, etc.
lack of privacy	privacy	bathrooms instead of curtained-off cubicles; single rooms offered; cubicles instead of dormitories; soundproofing in GPs' surgeries
creating dependence	supporting independence	physical aides to mobility; physical and electronic aids to communication; signposts to departments and wards; labels on doors; maps; easy access to telephones
Non-clinical routines		
rigid	flexible	patient choice of getting up and going to bed; of whether to sit by bed or in day room; of time of snack; demand or schedule feeding for babies
imposed	negotiable	choice of date and time of day for in-patient admission; choice of sessions at psychiatric day hospital; choice of dates for respite care
batch	individual	individual appointment in OPD, not block booking; choices from menu not set meal
closed	open	unrestricted visiting; parent accompanies child to anaesthetic and recovery rooms; relations help in care; woman's choice of companions in labour
Practitioner–patient interaction and communication		
impersonal	personal	'personal doctor' retained for patients in GP's group practices; continuity of care – same small group of midwives see

continued

Table 11.1—continued

From	To	Examples
Practitioner–patient interaction and communication		
		woman throughout pregnancy, labour and post-partum period; same doctor in out-patients departments; same physiotherapist each visit to department; primary nursing instead of task nursing; numbers of staff children and elderly patients see kept to minimum
autocratic	consultative relation- ships	patients take part in drawing up nursing care plans; informed choice of treatment rather than informed consent; in domiciliary care, patient or relation take lead in saying what help is needed
inducing dependency	supporting autonomy	information; explanation; seeking patients' values, views and priorities; patients' status as adult recognized
Clinical care		
care in institution	care at home	antenatal rest; paediatric care; some acute and orthopaedic care; care of dying; GP instead of consultant care
in-patients	day-patients	surgery; chemotherapy; diagnostic tests
long in-patient stays	shorter stays	psychiatry; post-natal stays; post-operative stays
severe physio- logical stress	less severe	shorter pre-operative fasting; local instead of general anaesthetic; 'key hole' surgery; more accurate dosages of medication; autologous blood transfusion; quicker return to normal drinking and eating; quicker mobilization
high psychologi- cal stress	lower stress	information about what to expect; support of relation; continuity of care; quicker return to self-care
higher risk	lower risk	non-invasive diagnostic procedures; more careful protocols regarding X-rays, CAT scans
curative care	preventive care	screening for pre-cancers; genetic counselling; early detection of correctable conditions; prevention of iatrogenesis, e.g. bedsores

SPECIFICATIONS FOR SERVICE AGREEMENTS

The reforms to the NHS introduced in *Working for Patients* included the instruction that specifications for services be drawn up between authorities providing health care and those purchasing it.[5] The purchasers are health authorities, responsible for meeting the health needs of the populations in their districts, and some general practitioners, those who hold funds to purchase treatment and care for their patients. Specifications for services create an opportunity for providers to offer, and purchasers to demand, high standards of treatment and care. To what levels of definition, in what detail and with what rigour those standards will be drawn up remains to be seen. Great though the opportunities are, they could be missed through tensions and conflicts of interest.

What is in the specifications?

The first area for tension is round the most basic point about specifications: what they include and omit. At the start of the new system, specification of standards has been slight and vague. It is likely that it will become more detailed in the next few years. After that, some of the detail may be replaced by reference to sets of standards covering part of a speciality or service. One set of NAWCH standards has already been included in some specifications (Chapter 6). MIND has been commissioned by the Department of Health to compile a set of standards for the care (but not the clinical treatment) of people with mental illness.[6] The Royal Colleges are engaged in the same work. The Royal College of Nursing, for example has compiled sets of standards for several care groups.[7] These are sound developments.

Professionals, however, particularly in provider organizations, will generally want the detailed specification of standards kept to a minimum. They will argue that specifying too much is stultifying and stops the development of new ways of doing things.[8] Consumerists will generally favour detailed specifications. They will suspect that professionals want freedom to fall below certain standards, as much as to rise above them. Corporate rationalizers will be caught between the two. But they will be drawn towards the professional preferences. That follows from the structural arguments in Chapter 2, as well as from corporate rationalizers' track record.

The status of standards

The second area for tension is to do with the status of what is specified. Standards can be categorized according to the degree of authority to be attributed to them. There are standards that must be complied with; guidelines that should be followed most of the time; and options that can be freely chosen.[9] Different health professionals view these differently. Doctors tend to see standards as absolute, requiring compliance. Nurses tend to interpret standards as guidelines to be worked towards.[10] Consumerists favour standards that are compulsory. Then they become in effect consumers' rights, provided that the consumers (or their relations) know what those standards are.[11] But both professionals and consumerists want flexibility retained for guidelines and options. So what are to be standards and what guidelines requires to be discussed during the drawing up of specifications. The status as well as the content of every standard specified needs to be made clear.

This clarity is especially important because the Department of Health has recently stepped back from setting national standards. It takes the view that 'It is for each health authority to decide the level of the service to be provided'.[12] The standards negotiated at national level between proto-professionals, consumerists and corporate rationalizers have been one of consumerists' best means of getting improvements locally. Their loss is a victory for dominant interest-holders and for some local corporate rationalizers, for both have long objected to national guidance from the Department.

The level of standards

Thirdly, the level at which standards are specified can be disputed, even when there is agreement about what are high standards. Standards for an issue or practice can be specified at any level between low and high. Different levels can have different costs in money, time, staff, space or other resources. The costs are sometimes incompletely known, or partly fall outside the provider or purchaser. High standards are not always dearer than lower ones. But corporate rationalizers may choose to offer or to purchase lower standards instead of higher, if they believe them to be cheaper. Professionals and consumerists are likely to be united in opposing that. They will think that more resources should be provided. Then consumers, allied with professionals, may come to exert a new influence on the government's policy of 'well planned inadequacy'.[13]

There may, however, be some standards that could be lowered without detriment to consumers. Then resources could be released to spend on other aspects of care and other higher standards. So there needs to be clarity about the costs and benefits of all standards in every speciality, service and health-care setting. There should be no pretence that a low standard is an 'optimal' or best one, if it is not. That means open discussion, with the opportunity for all interest groups to contribute to the analyses. Those analyses and discussions will be exacting.

These tensions and conflicts will make demands upon all the groups working on the specifications and contributing to them in other ways. Of particular importance will be the position adopted by GP fund-holders. The standards they press for are likely to be granted. So their potential power is great.

New demands

The professional bodies drawing up sets of standards (it is a reiterative process) would benefit from inviting one or two consumerists to work with them. Dominant interests would hardly topple. But consumerists' approach to standards could help professionals articulate more standards that are synergistic between professionals and consumers. The Royal College of General Practitioners has a Patients' Liaison Group of professional and lay members who discuss standards.[14] Local pressure and self-help groups could work with local professional groups in the same way. The idea of partnership finds its particular and most important expression in the patient–practitioner relationship. But it would be strengthened if it were reflected at all levels of the service.

Consumer pressure groups and consumerists also need to be ready to respond to the new challenges. Consumer groups can be confused in their identification of interests. They can too easily accept dominant interest-holders' definitions of consumers' interests. Articulating and pressing for non-synergistic interests is hard work politically. It is hard emotionally, too. Destroying consensus and opposing dominant interests can make those who do it feel guilty. If they wish to be accepted by dominant interest-holders and corporate rationalizers, it can go against their self-interest. Pressure groups and self-help groups with limited objectives can find unity of purpose. But groups with wider aims, attracting disparate members, can slip into supporting dominant interests non-synergistic with those they should be supporting. Community Health Councils are particularly at risk of confusion and ineffectiveness. That is because their members are appointed by outside bodies (Regional Health Authorities and Local Authorities), not self-selected. The wide variation in CHCs' performance comes chiefly from members' differences in alignment with dominant or repressed interests.[15] When members are predominantly aligned with dominant interests, they promote synergistic interests. When they are predominantly aligned with repressed interests, they work as radical CHCs. What should be their alignments? That question requires more analysis within CHCs and other consumer groups than it has had.

Another challenge to consumer groups is their attitude to clinical treatment and care. Many groups are reluctant to examine them or comment. But the boundaries between non-clinical care, collective clinical care and clinical care in the strict sense are not fixed (Chapter 2). The work of AIMS and NCT in maternity care shows that any assumption that technical clinical care is more likely than non-clinical care to be synergistic with consumers' interests is unsafe. In surgery, for example, different techniques for the same procedure can have different consequences for painfulness.[16] Some doctors and nurses are slow to adopt, or to drop, treatments shown by clinical trials to be effective, or ineffective.[17] Clinical trials can fail to ask patients what they feel and think. 'Feeling better', so important to patients, may escape research workers' notice.[18] Leaving topics like these unexamined supports dominant interests that are non-synergistic with repressed interests.

Corporate rationalizers and their challenging interests are also called to the contest by the new system. They, like many consumerists, have been slow to think about clinical care.[19] They are beginning to concern themselves with it now.[20] But further attention needs to be given to specifying high standards of non-clinical care of the kinds discussed in the chapters on support, respect, control and choice. These are not the superficial 'customer' or 'charm-school-and-better-wallpaper' aspects of provision that have engaged managers in recent years.[21] They are an essential part of health care. In addition, many consumerist standards for non-clinical care are well developed and validated. To test them in repeated patient satisfaction surveys wastes resources. Moreover, it fails to disclose suppressed interests.

In general, corporate rationalizers are tempted to challenge dominant interest-holders too little. Sometimes corporate rationalizers attribute obscurantism or recalcitrance to dominant interest-holders unjustly. Professionals not only come to accept higher standards. They also come to wonder why they did not do so sooner. Remembering that may help corporate rationalizers ensure that the trends towards higher standards are steadily and imaginatively pursued.

CONCLUSION

The moment of the rose and the moment of the yew-tree
Are of equal duration.

T. S. Eliot[1]

The conflicts between consumerists and professionals are disputes
about whose definitions of interest shall prevail. They hinge on
autonomy, just as do the struggles between individual patients and
practitioners. The consumerist claim that consumers can act in their
own best interests conflicts with the professional claim that those
interests can only be defined and assessed by professionals. At its
most polarized, that is a conflict over autonomy. Interests are the
counters of debate, the black-and-white chequers pushed across the
board, as well as its substance. In almost all disagreements between
consumerists and professionals one or the other, or both, invoke the
best interests of consumers to justify their views. We have moved on
from the times when it was enough for a practitioner to assert that
something was, or was not, in patients' best interests to end every
exchange. But we have not yet reached the times when it is enough
for a consumerist to assert it. Something in the way of argument or
evidence is rightly required. From this point in the discussion, let us
look again at health gains and at autonomy.

Health care is to do with gains in health. Those gains include gains
to the work-object and transcendence over it. They are facilitated
by well-judged work on the work-object and proper regard for the
person-subject. Professional standards should be based on a
reasonable theoretical rationale, empirical evidence and demonstrable gains in health. When those conditions are met (or at least
when they are not denied), professionals' preference for the *status
quo* is soundly based. It forms the store of expertise, experience,
care and concern that has brought about innumerable synergies of

interest between consumers and professionals. But the work and experiences of consumer groups and proto-professionals lead to three provisos.

The first is that once consumers or consumerists begin to express disquiet about specific practices or standards, professionals and managers should heed that disquiet. Consumerists' and consumers' feelings, insights and the conclusions they draw from their experiences always deserve attention. Where they conflict with current professional standards, research should be started early to try to find out where benefits to health (immediate, short term and long term) lie. Consumerists and proto-professionals should be invited to contribute to the research protocols. This is important because research is not value-free. It tends to carry dominant interests into its design and execution (as we saw in Chapter 3). The imperative to undertake research applies both to established practices and standards (as were restricted visiting for children or preventing parents from seeing their stillborn babies) and to new introductions (like the routine use of obstetric interventions). It is an abuse of dominant interest-holders' power to maintain, and especially to extend, standards that consumers or consumerists have questioned, unless the appropriate research is set in train.

The second proviso is that, once it has been demonstrated that changing a practice or standard would benefit consumers' health, professionals should feel an obligation to resist no longer. That obligation should be considered part of the very meaning of professionalism.

The third proviso is that professional standards cannot be 'owned' by professionals: standards affect consumers, and beyond them, other citizens. Consumers' ownership of standards that affect their welfare, their health and their lives is as great – or as little – as professionals'. Ideas for standards and about the health gains they are intended to secure come from many sources. The opening up of treatment and care to wider social influences, and to those from disciplines and areas of expertise outside medicine and nursing, is one of consumerism's benefits to health care. No single discipline can meet the therapeutic purposes, the moral complexities or the ethical dilemmas of health care on its own. Every standard is an expression of values; and those values are to do with us all.

Turning to autonomy, it can be argued that it and its supporters can be positive goods for consumers and professionals rather than in competition between them. Each's autonomy can be respected in some sense that acknowledges connectedness and common humanity. Respect between person-subjects can be mutual. Respect for the work-object can be shared. Information increases the understanding of those who give it as well as of those who receive it. Helping relations support patients enlarges practitioners' sensibilities and gives them privileged experiences of human relationships. Interactive control is part of all social encounters, and the norms governing it in health care settings can be modified to be less oppressive for consumers. Choice of something that affects the recipient more than the donor is offered in many 'ordinary' situations; health care is of greater significance than most of them. Making decisions about complex or uncertain matters benefits from the perspectives of both practitioner and patient. That the patient's decision should be fully informed and willing rather than made by default or from coercion is a basic ethic of medicine itself.[2] It needs to be strengthened there and brought in explicitly to nursing and paramedical practice. Although many professionals and many consumers are unpractised in the negotiations that favour the positive rather than the negative expressions of autonomy, there are enough exceptions to give hope that changes will continue to be made. Interests can be brought closer: good feeling, intelligence and justice can do it.

In coming to an optimistic conclusion, the protracted conflicts between consumerists or proto-professionals and professionals should not be forgotten. The distress that consumers feel when their interests are oppressed must be recognized with sorrow. The chilling disillusionment that consumers experience when they realize that their interests, or those of their relations, have been suppressed must be recalled with shame. So must the guilt and regret of practitioners who come to realize that what they believed was to patients' good was to their harm. Remembered, too, must be the achievements of professionals who have managed to redefine their view of consumers' interests. Relinquishing belief in the rightness of one practice or standard and replacing it with something that may be almost the opposite is hard for anyone. It is especially hard for professionals, for they invest themselves generously and intensely in their actions. To change those actions they have to change themselves. Anna Freud said something about courage that at first sight applies to consumers' fears of professionals' retaliatory powers. But it applies also to professionals' fears that consumers will deny professionals' expertise and destroy their power to do good:[2]

> What we call 'courage' in ordinary language is, I believe, no more than an individual's ability to deal with external threats on their own ground and prevent the bulk of them from joining forces with the manifold dangers lurking in the [unconscious].

The apple tree bears red, yellow and green apples. Eventually most will ripen to the rosy fruit of synergistic interests. But so long as the tree lives and flowers, there will always be a succession of unripe and half-ripe apples. That is the way things are. It is the task of everyone in the health service to try to hasten the ripening of the green and yellow apples.

REFERENCES AND NOTES

Chapter 1   Interests and ideologies

1 Brody, H. (1987). *Stories of Sickness*. New Haven, Yale University Press, p. 3. The moral and ethical basis of health care professional practice is discussed in Pellegrino, E. D. and Thomasma, D. C. (1981). *A Philosophical Basis of Medical Practice*. Oxford, Oxford University Press.

2 Beeforth, M. *et al*. (1990). *Whose Service is it Anyway?* London, Research and Development for Psychiatry, p. 9.

3 Miller, E.J. (1979). 'Autonomy, dependency and organisational change', in D. Towell and C. Harries (eds) *Innovation in Patient Care*. London, Croom Helm, pp. 180, 181.

4 Sedgwick, P. (1982). *Psycho Politics*. London, Pluto Press, p. 213.

5 Hughes, E.C. (1958). *Men and Their Work*. Glencoe, Ill., The Free Press, pp. 119–20.

6 Goffman, E. (1961). *Asylums*. New York, Doubleday and Co.

7 Alford, R.R. (1975). *Health Care Politics*. Chicago, University of Chicago Press. Alford has a third category of interests, challenging interests, held by managers and the government. Those interests are picked up in Chapter 2.

8 Warrington Community Health Council (1987). *Report of Survey into Visiting Arrangements at the District General Hospital*. Warrington, CHC, p. 10. Patients were asked if they preferred visiting from 7–8 p.m. or 7.30–8.30 p.m. per day.

9 Brody, loc. cit., p. 185, summarizing Eliot Freidson (see below).

10 Alford, loc. cit., p. 17.

11 Haug, M. and Sussman, M. (1969). 'Professional autonomy and the revolt of the client', *Social Problems*, 17, 153–61. They suggest that patients began to revolt against professionals because of their attempted control over aspects of the patients' lives and care that lay beyond professionals' proper concern, and because of incompetent or mistaken

efforts within their proper concern. This is a useful way at looking at consumerism's origins – in my metaphor the snake should have stayed on the staff, imparting wisdom to the doctor, rather than crawling away into the grass, where he bit the daughter of Eve. But it will not do for the continuation of consumerism because it omits suppressed interests.

12 Department of Health and Social Security and Welsh Office (1976). *The Organisation of the In-Patient's Day*. London, HMSO, p. 17.
13 Kitzinger, S. (1979). *The Good Birth Guide*. Glasgow, Fontana Paperbacks, p. 454.
14 Maternity Services Advisory Committee (1985). *Maternity Care in Action*, Part 111. London, HMSO, p. 6.
15 Lukes, S. (1974). *Power*. London, Macmillan.
16 Boon, N.A. (1991). 'New deal for old hearts', *British Medical Journal*, 303, 70.
17 Aaron, H.J. and Schwartz, W.B. (1984). *The Painful Prescription*. Washington, D.C., The Brookings Institution.
18 Boon, loc. cit.
19 Total Quality Management, a management technique from industry now being widely adopted in the health service, emphasizes improving interdisciplinary and management systems within organizations, in order to deliver better care. It has great potential but as yet is insufficiently directed towards meeting consumerists' and consumers' standards.
20 Williamson, C. (1988). 'Dominant, challenging and repressed interests in the NHS', *Health Services Management*, 84, 170–4.
21 Lukes, loc cit., p. 34.
22 Sontag, S. (1988). *Illness as Metaphor*. New York, Anchor Books, p. 3. (First published 1987.)
23 Sontag, loc. cit., pp. 17–20.
24 Standards are often discussed in terms of structure, what resources are used and how they are organized (this includes staff); process, how what is provided is used and the ways care and treatment are given; and outcome, gains or losses to patients' health and satisfaction. Donabedian, A. (1980). *Explorations in Quality Assessment and Monitoring, vol. 1, The Definition of Quality and Approaches to its Assessment*. Michigan, Ann Arbor, Health Administration Press.
25 Chapman, G.E. (1983). 'Ritual and rational action in hospitals', *Journal of Advanced Nursing*, 8, 13–20.
26 Menzies, I.E.P. (1959). 'The functioning of social systems as a defence against anxiety', *Human Relations*, 13, 95–121.
27 Williamson, C. (1986). 'Authority members and Standards of non-clinical care', *Hospital and Health Services Review*, 82, 18–23.
28 McCullough, L.B. (1988). 'An ethical model for improving the patient–physician relationship', *Inquiry*, 25, 454–68. '[the physician's]

moral obligation [is] to protect and promote the best interests of the patient . . .'

29 Freidson, E. (1970). *Profession of Medicine*. New York, Dodd, Mead, pp. 137–57.

Chapter 2   Consumerists

1 Trilling, L. (1970). *The Liberal Imagination*. Harmondsworth, Peregrine Books, p. 11.

2 Hogg, C. (1988). *Frontier Medicine*. London, Greater London Association of CHCs, p. 54.

3 Klein, R. and Lewis, J. (1976). *The Politics of Consumer Representation*. London, Centre for Studies in Social Policy, p. 17.

4 Bowlby, J. (1973). *Separation*. Harmondsworth, Penguin Books, p. 186.

5 Wilson-Barnett, J. (1989). 'Limited autonomy and partnership: professional relationships in health care', *Journal of Medical Ethics*, 15, 12–16.

6 Radical Statistics Health Group (1980). *The Unofficial Guide to Official Health Statistics*. London, Radical Statistics, p. 4.

7 Hoffenberg, R. (1987). *Clinical Freedom*. London, Nuffield Provincial Hospitals Trust.

8 Williamson, C. (1990). 'Authority members and standards of clinical care', *Health Services Management*, 86, 26–8.

9 AIMS (1990). *What is AIMS?* London, Association for Improvements in the Maternity Services.

10 Belson, P. (1990). Personal communication. Mrs Belson was a founder member of NAWCH.

11 The Patients Association (n.d.). *The Voice of the Patient*. London, Patients Association.

12 Bowlby, J. (1952). *Maternal Care and Mental Health*. Geneva, World Health Organization.

13 Winnicott, D.W. (1964). *The Child, the Family and the Outside World*. Harmondsworth, Penguin Books.

14 Psychoanalytic theory, influential in the 1960s, has been in part superseded by attachment theory – see Bowlby, J. (1988). *A Secure Base*. London, Routledge.

15 These issues are taken from the NAWCH journal *Update* over the years 1970 to 1990. In the last year or so, NAWCH has begun to take up a few clinical issues.

16 Shelley, P. (1989). 'Conference round-up', *Update*, 28, 7.

17 For examples see Jobling, R. (1977). 'Learning to live with it: an account of a career of chronic dermatological illness and patienthood', in A. Davis and G. Horobin (eds) *Medical Encounters*. London, Croom

Helm, pp. 72–86; and Oliver, M. (1990). *The Politics of Disablement*. Basingstoke, Macmillan Education.

18 Macintyre, S. and Oldman, D. (1977). 'Coping with migraine', in Davis and Horobin, loc. cit., pp. 55–71.

19 AIMS, loc. cit. (1990).

20 Stewart, N. (1988). *AIMS Quarterly Journal*, 2, p. 3.

21 Yorkshire Regional Health Authority (1991). *Draft Policy, Caring for Mothers and Babies in Yorkshire*. Harrogate, Yorkshire RHA, p. 6.

22 Fretwell, J.E. (1980). 'Hospital ward routine – friend or foe?', *Journal of Advanced Nursing*, 5, 625–636.

23 NAWCH (1987). *Update*, 20, Spring, p. 8.

24 Beech, B. (1982). *AIMS Quarterly Journal*, Summer, p. 1.

25 AIMS (1987). *AIMS Quarterly Journal*, Autumn, p. 12.

26 Alford, R.R. (1975). *Health Care Politics*. Chicago, University of Chicago press, pp. 190–4.

27 Williamson, C. (1988). 'Dominant, challenging and repressed interests in the NHS', *Health Services Management*, 84, 170–4.

28 *Shorter Oxford English Dictionary*.

29 Department of Health and Social Security (1979). *Patients First*. London, HMSO.

30 NAWCH (1990). 'Income and Expenditure Account for the Year Ended 31 December 1989', *Annual Report*. London, National Association for the Welfare of Children in Hospital.

31 Honorary Treasurer, AIMS (1990). Personal communication.

32 Key, E. (1992). Personal communication. Mrs Key is Honorary Publications Secretary of AIMS.

33 Ministry of Health (1959). *The Welfare of Children in Hospital*. London, HMSO.

34 Fox-Russell, P. (1991). Personal communication. Dr Fox-Russell was an early member of AIMS and gave it medical advice.

35 Ministry of Health (1961). *Human Relations in Obstetrics*. London, HMSO, p. 4.

36 This is evident in – for example – the sets of standards published in 1990 by the Royal College of Nursing. Standards are there defined as 'A professionally agreed level of performance'. *Standards of Care, Paediatric Nursing*. Harrow, Scutari Press, p. ix.

37 Jean Baker Miller makes the same point about women *vis-à-vis* men in *Toward a New Psychology of Women* (1976). Boston, Beacon Press, p. 10.

Chapter 3   Consumerists' and consumers' standards

1 Camus, A. (1961). *Resistance, Rebellion and Death*. New York, Alfred A. Knopf, p. 240.

2 Riley, E.M.D. (1977). 'What do women want? – The question of choice

in the conduct of labour', in T. Chard and M. Richards (eds) *Benefits and Hazards of The New Obstetrics*. London, Spastics International Medical Publications, p. 68.

3 Robinson, J. (1975). Personal communication. Mrs Robinson was chair of The Patients Association.

4 Rogers, A. and Pilgrim, D. (1991). 'Pulling down churches: accounting for the British Mental Health Users' Movement', *Sociology of Health and Illness*, 13, 129–47.

5 Hemmings, G. (1989). *Inside Schizophrenia*. London, Sidgwick & Jackson, p. 73.

6 Nelson, M.K. (1983). 'Working-class women, middle-class women, and models of childbirth', *Social Problems*, 30, 284–97.

7 Nelson, loc. cit.

8 Cartwright, A. (1979). *The Dignity of Labour?* London, Tavistock Publications, p. 114.

9 East Dorset CHC (1987). *Christchurch Hospital, Survey of Needs, Expectations and Priorities of Outpatients*. Wessex RHA and East Dorset Community Health Council. In using examples from this survey, I imply no criticism of it. It is better than many surveys; and in any case neither a need, nor an expectation nor a priority is the same as a standard.

10 York District Health Authority (1985). Unpublished paper. This is an example of research carried out after staff had opposed change. Both the research and the change were successfully completed but caused consternation to dominant interest-holders.

11 Caple, T. and Deigham, Y. (1986). *Managing Customer Relations, The Customers' Agenda*. London, N.W. Thames RHA, p. 11.

12 Caple, T. and Deigham, Y. (1986). *Managing Customer Relations, Taking a Snapshot*. N.W. Thames RHA, unpaginated.

13 Kitzinger, S. (1975). *Some Mothers' Experiences of Induced Labour*. London, National Childbirth Trust.

14 Oakley, A. and Richards, M. (1990). 'Women's Experiences of Caesarian Delivery', in J. Garcia *et al.* (ed.) *The Politics of Maternity Care*. Oxford, Clarendon Press, pp. 184–97.

15 Tew, M. (1990). *Safer Childbirth?* London, Chapman and Hall, pp. 120–2.

16 Kitzinger, loc. cit.

17 The Royal College of Midwives (1991). *Towards a Healthy Nation*. London, RCM.

18 Welsh Office NHS Directorate (1991). *Maternal and Early Child Health*. Cardiff, Welsh Office, p. 35.

19 The Audit Commission is beginning to enquire into consumers' experiences of clinical care, as in *Measuring Quality: The Patient's View of Day Surgery* (1991). The Audit Commission for Local Authorities and the NHS in England and Wales, London, HMSO.

20 After this book had gone to press, the Health Committee of the House of Commons published a report largely supporting consumerist standards and aspirations for the maternity services, as expressed to the Committee by AIMS, NCT and other organizations and individuals. House of Commons Health Committee (1992) *Second Report, Maternity Services Vol. I.* London, HMSO.

21 Pritchard, P.M.M. (1981). 'Patient participation in primary health care: a discussion paper', in P. Pritchard (ed.) *Patient Participation in General Practice.* London, Royal College of General Practitioners.

22 Beeforth, M. *et al.* (eds) (1990). *Whose Service is it Anyway?* London, Research and Development for Psychiatry, p. 10.

23 Graffy, J.P. (1981). 'Patient participation in primary health care', in Pritchard (ed.), loc. cit.

24 Beeforth *et al.*, loc. cit.

25 Barker, I. (1991). 'Purchasing for people', *Health Services Management*, 87, 212–14.

26 Welsh Office (1978). *Standards of Care for Mentally Ill and Mentally Handicapped Patients in Hospital.* Cardiff, Welsh Office, pp. 12, 14.

27 Anon. (1986). 'A personal report', *Patient Voice*, Spring, pp. 2, 3.

28 Macfarlane, A. (1985). 'When givers prove unkind', *Nursing Mirror*, 161, 36, 37.

29 Davis, F. (1975). 'Professional socialization as a subjective experience: the process of doctrinal conversion among student nurses', in C. Cox and A. Mead (eds) *A Sociology of Medical Practice.* London, Collier-Macmillan, pp. 116–31.

30 Dennison, A. (1989). 'Knowledge, belief and hope', *British Medical Journal*, 298, 1589.

31 McKenzie, A. (1989). 'A View from the Bed', *Nursing Times*, 86, 55.

32 Wooff, D. (1988). 'From the other side of the fence', *British Medical Journal*, 297, 1417.

33 Gray, C.S. (1989). 'Shared care must be accountable', *British Medical Journal*, 298, 763.

34 Lautmann, B. (1989). 'Them and us', *Nursing Times*, 85, 41.

35 Anon. (1990). 'Reflections after manic depressive psychosis', *British Medical Journal*, 300, 1597.

Chapter 4   Autonomy and therapeutic benefits

1 Berlin, I. (1969). *Four Essays on Liberty*. London, Oxford University Press. p. 131.

2 Miller, J.B. (1976). *Towards a New Psychology of Women*. Boston, Beacon Press.

3 Bowlby, J. (1988). *A Secure Base*. London, Routledge, p. 27.

4 Psychoanalytic ideas give us ways of expressing our deepest feelings.

For the infant self, see Klein, M. (1959). 'Our adult world and its roots in infancy', *Human Relations*, 12, 291–303.

5 Diemert, S. (1990). 'Health within the experience of breast cancer', *Journal of Advanced Nursing*, 15, 1426–35.

6 Simpson, M. *et al.* (1991). 'Doctor – patient communication: the Toronto consensus statement', *British Medical Journal*, 303, 1385–7.

7 Stimson, G.V. (1974). 'Obeying doctor's orders: a view from the other side', *Social Science and Medicine*, 8, 97–104.

8 Bradley, C.P. (1992). 'Uncomfortable prescribing decisions', *British Medical Journal*, 304, 294–46.

Chapter 5   Respect

1 Jolley, M.G. (1988). 'Ethics of cancer management from the patient's perspective', *Journal of Medical Ethics*, 14, 188–90.

2 Ferguson, M. (1988). 'The person inside the patient', *Nursing Times*, 84, 40.

3 Gadow, S. (1980). 'Body and self: a dialectic', *Journal of Medicine and Philosophy*, 5, 172–85.

4 Foucault, M. (1973). *The Birth of the Clinic*. London, Tavistock Publications. (First published in France in 1963.)

5 Gould, S.J. (1991). *Bully for Brontosaurus*. London, Hutchinson Radius, pp. 473–8.

6 Patients are work objects in two senses: objects worked on, and the practitioner's livelihood. The latter strongly influences the organization of professions and professional work, with ensuing advantages and detriments to consumers. See Gerson, E.M. (1976). 'The social character of illness: deviance or politics?', *Social Science and Medicine*, 10, 219–24. I am using it in this chapter on the first sense.

7 An eminent York GP.

8 Models of the doctor–patient interaction envisage a continuum of reciprocal contributions from patient passive/doctor active to patient active/doctor passive. Friedson, E. (1975). *Profession of Medicine*. New York, Dodd, Mead, pp. 315–21. The four tasks fit onto this continuum, and extend it, though they are four – rather than double – stranded. Patients' work does not cease when they are unconscious, because they can retain some awareness and memory of what happens. Practitioners' work only ceases when the practitioner ceases thinking about that patient.

9 Alderson, P. (1990). *Choosing for Children*. Oxford, Oxford University Press, pp. 41, 42.

10 Evers, H.K. (1981). 'The creation of patient careers in geriatric wards', *Social Science and Medicine*, 15A, 581–7. Lack of techniques for treatment have also prevented nurses from helping people with severe

mental handicaps. Now called 'people with learning difficulties', they are best taught and cared for outside the health service.

11 Menzies, I.E.P. (1959). 'The functioning of social systems as a defence against anxiety', *Human Relations*, 13, 95–121.

12 Siegel, B.S. (1989). *Peace, Love & Healing*. New York, Harper Row, p. 130.

13 Work on the work-object and for the person-subject is sometimes split between two practitioners – a doctor and a nurse, say. But this is probably only fairly satisfactory to many patients.

14 Wilkinson, C. (1990). 'Postnatal euphoria', *British Medical Journal*, 301, 558.

15 Nyman, J. (1989). 'Fighting the nightmare', *Nursing Times*, 85, 53.

16 Katz, P. and Kirkland, F.R. (1988). 'Traditional thought and modern surgery', *Social Science and Medicine*, 26, 1175–81.

17 James, A. (1990). 'Why perpetuate the shaving ritual?' *Nursing Times*, 86, 37, 38.

18 Walsh, M. and Ford, P. (1989). *Nursing Rituals*. Oxford, Heinemann Nursing.

19 Dootson, S. (1990). 'Sensory imbalance and sleep loss', *Nursing Times*, 86, 26, 29.

20 Beeforth, M. *et al.* (1990). *Whose Service is it Anyway?* London, Research and Development in Psychiatry, p. 29.

21 Seen in an acute geriatric ward, 1990.

22 Speedling, E.J. and Rosenberg, G. (1986). 'Patient well-being: a responsibility for hospital managers', *Health Care Management Review*, 11, 9–19.

23 MIND (1987). *Visiting a Psychiatric Hospital*. London, National Association for Mental Health, duplicated paper.

24 Homan, R. (1986). 'Observations on the management of mood in a neurological hospital', *British Medical Journal*, 293, 1417–19.

25 Pearson, A. (1989). *Primary Nursing*. London, Chapman and Hall, pp. 125–42.

26 Watson, C. (1987). 'Portrait study', *Nursing Times*, 83, 64–67.

27 Taylor, C. (1970). *In Horizontal Orbit*. New York, Holt, Rinehart and Winston, pp. 78–80.

Chapter 6 Support

1 Hawker, R. (1985). 'A day in the life of a patient', *Nursing Times*, 81, 43, 44.

2 Observed in a surgical ward, 1983.

3 Delight, E. and Goodall, J. (1990). *Love and Loss*. London, MacKeith Press, p. 24.

4 Benner, P. and Wrubel, J. (1989). *The Primacy and Caring*. Menlo Park, California, Addison-Wesley.

5 Robertson, J. and Robertson, J. (1989). *Separation and the Very Young*. London, Free Association Books, pp. 1–4.
6 The films were made in 1951 and 1954, Robertson loc. cit., pp. 26–57.
7 Suttie, I.D. (1960). *The Origins of Love and Hate*. Harmondsworth, Penguin Books. (First published in 1935.)
8 Bowlby, J. (1951). *Maternal Care and Mental Health*. Geneva, World Health Organization.
9 Harlow, H.F. and M.K. (1961). 'A study of animal affection', *Natural History*, 70, 48–55. The Harlows conducted experiments in rearing monkeys from 1958 to 1962. The separation of infant and mother monkeys is now regarded as so cruel that a special licence from the Home Office is required to do any research that involves it.
10 Brain, D.J. and Maclay, I. (1968). 'Controlled study of mothers and children in hospital', *British Medical Journal*, i (5587), 278–80.
11 For paediatric wards: MacCarthy, D. *et al.* (1968). 'The handling of the sick child', in J. Gould (ed.) *The Prevention of Damaging Stress in Children*. London, J. & A. Churchill, pp. 1–23. For SCBUs: Kennell, J.H. and Klaus, M.H. (1976). *Parent–Infant Bonding*. St Louis, C.V. Mosby.
12 MacCarthy, D. and MacKeith, R. (1965). 'A parent's voice', *Lancet*, ii 18 December, 1289–91.
13 Taylor, M.R.H. and O'Connor, P. (1989). 'Resident parents and shorter hospital stay', *Archives of Diseases in Childhood*, 64, 274–6.
14 NAWCH (1989). *NAWCH Quality Review*. London, National Association for the Welfare of Children in Hospital, p. 9.
15 Department of Health (1991). *Welfare of Children and Young People in Hospital*. London, HMSO, p. 16.
16 Association of CHCs in England and Wales (1986). *Patients' Charter*. London, ACHCEW.
17 Middlemiss, M. (1979). *Nursing Times*, 75, 1228. [Letter]
18 Alderson, P. (1983). *Special Care for Babies in Hospital*. London, National Association for the Welfare of Children in Hospital, p. 65.
19 Delight and Goodall, loc. cit., p. 28.
20 Delight and Goodall, loc. cit. p. 48.

Chapter 7   Information

1 Jolley, M.G. (1988). 'Ethics of cancer management from the patient's perspective', *Journal of Medical Ethics*, 14, 188–90.
2 Brearley, S. (1990). *Patient Participation*. Harrow, Scutari Press, pp. 39–42.
3 AIMS (1991). Submission to the House of Commons Health Committee, Part II. Association for Improvements in the Maternity Services, unpublished paper, p. 26.

4 Tuckett, D. *et al.* (1985). *Meetings Between Experts*. London, Tavistock, p. 206.

5 Barber, B. (1980). *Informed Consent in Medical Therapy and Research*. New Jersey, Rutgers University Press, p. 37.

6 Juul Jensen, U. and Mooney, G. (1990). 'Changing values: autonomy and paternalism in medicine and health care', in J. Jensen and Mooney (eds) *Changing Values in Medical Health Care Decision Making*. Chichester, John Wiley, pp. 1–15.

7 ACHCEW (1986). *Patients' Charter*. London, Association of Community Health Councils of England and Wales.

8 Bradford DHA (1990). Draft service specification. Unpublished paper.

9 Jones, J.S. (1981). 'Telling the right patient', *British Medical Journal*, 283–291–2.

10 Dennison, J.A.G. (1988). *British Medical Journal*, 297, 1192. [Letter]

11 Charlton, B.G. (1991). 'Stories of sickness', *British Journal of General Practice*, 41, 222–3.

12 Everett, C.B. and Preece, F.E. (1987). *British Medical Journal*, 295, 1281. [Letter]

13 Moss, T. (1990). Personal communication. Dr Moss is a consultant in genitourinary medicine.

14 Vallely, S.R. and Manton Mills, J.O. (1990). 'Should radiologists talk to patients?', *British Medical Journal*, 300, 3905–6.

15 Ford, A. (1990). 'Patients are worms', *Nursing Times*, 86, 59.

16 Nursing Development Units are wards where nurses are in charge of policy and seek to develop excellent practice. Such nurses are likely to be proto-professionals.

17 I am indebted to Mr John Porter for showing me this ward in 1991.

18 Maybury, J.F. *et al.* (1987). 'Information assessment by patients of a booklet on achalasia and its effect on anxiety levels', *Public Health,* 101, 119–22.

19 Kohner, N. (1989). *Information for People with Arthritis*. London, Arthritis Care, p. 15.

20 Pfeffer, N. and Quick, A. (1988). *Infertility Services*. London, Greater London Association of Community Health Councils, pp. 40–5.

21 Mendel, D. (1984). *Proper Doctoring*. Berlin, Springer-Verlag, pp. 75–6.

22 Devine, E. and Cook, T. (1986). 'Clinical and cost-saving effects of psychoeducational interventions with surgical patients: A meta analysis', *Research in Nursing and Health*, 9, 89–105.

23 Hathaway, D. (1986). 'Effect of pre-operative instruction on post-operative outcomes: A meta-analysis', *Nursing Research*, 35, 269–75.

24 Janis, I.L. (1958). *Psychological Stress*. New York, J. Wiley.

25 Ridgeway, V. and Mathews, A. (1982). 'Psychological preparation for surgery: a comparison of methods', *British Journal of Clinical Psychology*, 21, 271–80.

26 Miller, S.M. *et al.* (1988). 'Styles of coping with threat: implications for health', *Journal of Personality and Social Psychology*, 54, 142–8.

Chapter 8   Control

1 Sites, P. (1973). *Control*. New York, Dunellen, p. 1.
2 Seligman, M.E.P. (1975). *Helplessness*. San Francisco, W.H. Freeman. Many studies of perceived lack of control fail to define and control variables adequately.
3 See references to this in Chapter 3.
4 Stockwell, F. (1972). *The Unpopular Patient*. London, Royal College of Nursing.
5 English, J. and Morse, J.M. (1988). 'The "difficult" elderly patient: adjustment or malajustment?', *International Journal of Nursing Studies*, 25, 23–39.
6 English and Morse, loc. cit.
7 Brossat, S. and Pinell, P. (1990). 'Coping with parents', *Sociology of Health and Illness*, 12, 69–83.
8 Trevelyan, J. (1988). 'Taking their own medicine', *Nursing Times*, 84, 28–32.
9 The Royal College of Surgeons of England and the College of Anaesthetists (1990). *Pain after Surgery*. London, RCSE/CoA, p. 3.
10 *The Times* (1991). 24 January.
11 *Journal Watch* (1991). 15 March, 1.
12 The Royal College and College of Anaesthetists, loc. cit., p. 3.
13 *The Independent* (1990). 30 October, 17.
14 Bischoff, U. (1987). 'From Edinburgh to Berlin', *Nursing Times*, 83, 34–5.
15 Told me by the mother, 1975.
16 Lovell, A. *et al.* (1986). *Why Not Give Mothers their Own Notes?* London, Cicely Northcote Trust.
17 Lovell, A. and Elbourne, D. (1987). 'Holding the baby – and your notes', *The Health Service Journal*, 97, 335.
18 Essex, B. *et al.* (1990). 'Pilot study of records of shared care for people with mental illnesses', *British Medical Journal*, 300, 1442–6.
19 Gill, M.W. and Scott, D.L. (1986). 'Can patients benefit from reading copies of their doctors' letters about them?', *British Medical Journal*, 293, 1278–9.
20 Lovell *et al.* loc. cit., p. 48.
21 Beeforth, M. *et al.* (1990). *Whose Service is it Anyway?* London, Research and Development for Psychiatry, p. 1.
22 Cobb, J. (1987). 'Bridging two worlds', *Community Outlook*, August, pp. 21–4.
23 Lovell *et al.* loc. cit., pp. 145, 143.
24 Flint, C. (1986). *Sensitive Midwifery*. London, Heinemann, p. 158.

25 Henley, A. and Kohner, N. (1991). *Guidelines for Professionals.* London, Stillbirth and Neonatal Death Society.

Chapter 9 Choice

1 Dixon, J.M. (1991). Personal communication.
2 See ref. 2, Chapter 8.
3 Slevin, M.L. *et al.* (1990). 'Attitudes to chemotherapy: comparing views of patients with cancer with those of doctors, nurses, and general public', *British Medical Journal*, 300, 1458–60.
4 Adelaide Medical Centre Primary Health Care Team (1991). 'A primary health care team manifesto', *British Journal of General Practice*, 41, 31–3.
5 City and Hackney CHC (1989). *Pregnancy and Birth in Hackney and the City of London.* London, City and Hackney CHC, p. 31.
6 Bamford, O. *et al.* (1990). 'Change for the better', *Nursing Times*, 86, 28–32.
7 Beeforth, M. *et al.* (1990). *Whose Service is it Anyway?* London, Research and Development for Psychiatry, p. 1.
8 Townsend, J. *et al.* (1990). 'Terminal cancer care and patients' preference for place of death', *British Medical Journal*, 301, 415–17. (One patient wanted to die 'elsewhere'.)
9 City and Hackney CHC, loc. cit., pp. 7–9.
10 City and Hackney CHC, loc. cit., p. 6.
11 James, J. (1990). 'The politics of user information', *New Generation*, December 6–7.
12 Informed consent includes the option to refuse treatment, except under certain legally-defined circumstances. But some professionals, perhaps inadvertently or unconsciously, play down the option of refusal.
13 Tew, M. (1990). *Safer Childbirth?* London, Chapman and Hall, pp. 180–97.
14 Department of Health official (1990). Personal communication.
15 Royal College of Midwives (1991). *Towards a Healthy Nation.* London, Royal College of Midwives.
16 Kitzinger, S. (1979). *The Good Birth Guide.* Glasgow, Fontana Paperbacks.
17 Kitziger, loc. cit., pp. 19, 20.
18 Kuester, G.F. and Wolfe, S.M. (1991). *HRG Report on Screening Mammography and Ranking of Eleven Metro Washington Area Facilities.* Washington, D.C., Public Citizen Health Research Group.
19 Royal College of Radiologists and the National Radiological Protection Board (1991). *Patient Dose Reduction in Diagnostic Radiology.* London, HMSO.
20 Consumers' Association (1991). 'X-rays', *Which?*, January, London, Consumers' Association Ltd, pp. 40, 41.

21 Goddard, A. and Bowling, A. (1987). 'An international comparison of health education literature on breast disorders', *Health Education Journal*, 46, 92.

22 Wilson, R.G. *et al.* (1988). 'Mastectomy or conservation: the patient's choice', *British Medical Journal*, 297, 1167–9.

23 Morris, J. and Ingham, R. (1988). 'Choice of surgery for early breast cancer: Psychological considerations', *Social Science and Medicine*, 27, 1257–62.

24 King's Fund (1986). *Treatment of Primary Breast Cancer, Consensus Statement.* London, King's Fund.

25 Dixon, J.M. (1991). Personal communication.

26 Fallowfield, L.J. *et al.* (1990). 'Psychological outcomes of different treatment policies in women with early breast cancer outside a clinical trial', *British Medical Journal*, 301, 575–80.

27 Chadwick, D.J. *et al.* (1991). 'Medical or surgical orchidectomy: the patients' choice', *British Medical Journal*, 302, 572.

Chapter 10   Decision-making

1 Gillett, G.R. (1989). 'Informed consent and moral integrity', *Journal of Medical Ethics*, 15, 117–23.

2 Anon. (1983). 'Impaired autonomy and rejection of treatment', *Journal of Medical Ethics*, 9, 131–2.

3 Lazare, A. *et al.* (1975). 'The customer approach to patienthood', *Archives of General Psychiatry*, 32, 553–8.

4 Harrison, A.T. (1987). 'Appointment Systems: feasibility study of a new approach', *British Medical Journal*, 294, 1465–6.

5 Reid, M. (1991). 'Health care menu', *Nursing Times*, 87, 32–4.

6 Lazare, loc. cit.

7 Eisenthal, S. and Lazare, A. (1976). 'Evaluation of the initial interview in a walk-in clinic. The patient's perspective on a 'customer approach', *Journal of Nervous and Mental Diseases*, 162, 169–76.

8 Macintyre, S. and Oldman, D. (1977). 'Coping with Migraine', in A. Davis and G. Horobin (eds) *Medical Encounters*. London, Croom Helm, pp. 55–71. There are many similar accounts for other chronic conditions.

9 Wilson-Barnett, J. (1989). 'Limited autonomy and partnership: professional relationships in health care', *Journal of Medical Ethics*, 15, 12–16.

10 Oliver, M. (1988). 'Flexible services', *Nursing Times*, 84, 25–29.

11 Stewart, K. and Rai, G. (1989). 'A matter of life and death', *Nursing Times*, 85, 27–9.

12 Dudley, N.J. (1990). *British Medical Journal*, 300, 1271. [Letter]

13 Annas, G.J. (1991). 'The health care proxy and the living will', *New England Journal of Medicine*, 324, 1210–13.

14 Emanuel, L.L. *et al.* (1991). 'Advance directives for medical care – a case for greater use', *New England Journal of Medicine*, 324, 889–95.
15 Danis, M. *et al.* (1991). 'A prospective study of advance directives for life-sustaining care', *New England Journal of Medicine*, 324, 882–8.
16 Annas, loc. cit.
17 The Natural Death Centre (1991). *What is the Natural Death Centre?* London, The Natural Death Centre.
18 Blanchard, C.G. *et al.* (1988). 'Information and decision-making preferences of hospitalized adult cancer patients', *Social Science and Medicine*, 27, 1139–45. 'Interactions' rather than patients were studied, so the number of patients is less than the number of interactions given (439), apparently 200.
19 Waterworth, S. and Luker, K.A. (1990). 'Reluctant collaborators: do patients want to be involved in decisions concerning care?', *Journal of Advanced Nursing*, 15, 971–6. This is a very small sample, but worth citing because of the patients' apprehension even in acute wards.
20 Waterworth, S. (1991). Personal communication.
21 Simpson, M. *et al.* (1991). 'Doctor–patient communication: the Toronto consensus statement', *British Medical Journal*, 303, 1385–7.
22 Mendel, D. (1984). *Proper Doctoring*. Berlin, Springer-Verlag, p. 42.
23 Fisher, S. and Dundas Todd, A. (eds) (1983). *The Social Organization of Doctor–Patient Communication*. Washington, D.C., Centre for Applied Linguistics.
24 Fisher, S. (1983). 'Doctor talk/patient talk: how treatment decisions are negotiated in doctor–patient communication', in Fisher and Todd, loc. cit., pp. 135–57.
25 Silverman, D. (1987). *Communication and Medical Practice*. London, Sage Publications, pp. 136–57.
26 Roter, D. (1987). 'An exploration of health education's responsibility for a partnership model of client–provider relations', *Patient Education and Counselling*, 9, 25–31.
27 The Patients' Liaison Committee of the Royal College of General Practitioners favours a partnership model. Bugler, D. (1990). *British Journal of General Practice*, 40, 261–2. [Letter]

Chapter 11 Standards and specifications

1 Meade, K. and Carter, T. (1990). 'Empowering older users', in L. Winn (ed.) *Power to the People*. London, King's Fund Centre, pp. 19–27.
2 Strauss, A. and Glaser, B. (1970). *Anguish*. San Francisco, Sociology Press.
3 Royal College of Nursing (1990). *Standards of Care for Paediatric Nursing*. Harrow, Scutari Press, p. 5.

4 Table extended from Williamson, C. (1987). *Reviewing the Quality of Care in the NHS*. Birmingham, National Association of Health Authorities and Trusts, pp. 7, 8.
5 Secretaries of State for Health, Wales, Scotland and Northern Ireland (1989). *Working for Patients*. London, HMSO.
6 Lucas, J. (1991). Personal communication. Ms Lucas is Developments Director for MIND.
7 For example, for orthopaedic nursing (1990); cancer nursing (1991) and ref. 3.
8 Williamson, C. (1990). 'Authority members and standards of clinical care', *Health Services Management*, 86, 78–70.
9 Eddy, D.M. (1990). 'Designing a practice policy, standards, guidelines and options', *Journal of the American Medical Association*, 263, 3077–84.
10 Kitson, A. (1991). Quoted in *Nursing Times*, 87, 23.
11 Winkler, F. (1990). *Who Protects the Consumer in Community Care?* London, Greater London Association of CHCs, p. 29.
12 Letter from Health Minister, Virginia Bottomley, 1991, to Patients Association, quoted in *Patient Voice*, 51, 8.
13 Grimes, D.S. (1989). 'The end of charity?', *British Medical Journal*, 299, 1170–1.
14 Dennis, N. (1988). 'A model for joint working', *Journal of the Royal College of General Practitioners*, November, 491.
15 Williamson, C. (1983). A study of the Lay Contribution to Standards of Non-clinical care. DPhil. thesis, University of York.
16 Armstrong, P.J. and Burgess, R.W. (1990). 'Choice of incision and pain following gall-bladder surgery', *British Journal of Surgery*, 77, 746–8.
17 O'Dowd, T.C. and Wilson, A.D. (1991). 'Set menus and clinical freedom', *British Medical Journal*, 303, 450–2.
18 Wynne, A. (1989). 'Is it any good? the evaluation of therapy by participants in a clinical trial', *Social Science and Medicine*, 29, 1289–97.
19 Harrison, S. *et al.* (1989). *General Management in the NHS, Before and After the White Paper*. Leeds, Nuffield Institute for Health Service Studies, p. 19.
20 Cook, H. (1991). 'Building clinical innovation into a trust', *News*, 51. London, NHS Management Executive, pp. 12–13.
21 Pollitt, C. (1988). 'Bringing consumers into performance management: concepts, consequences and constraints', *Policy and Politics*, 16, 77–87.

Chapter 12   Conclusion

1 Eliot, T.S. (1944). 'Little Gidding', in *Four Quartets*. London, Faber and Faber.
2 Freud, A. (1965). Comments in *The Psychoanalytic Study of the Child*, 11, 432.

INDEX